Midwifery for The Soul

Awaken to Your Fierce Feminine in The Depths of Darkness and Trauma

Shared Wisdom Through Prose, Poetry, and Philosophy

JENNIFER SUMMERFELDT, MACP

Jennifer Summerfeldt/JS Coaching

Edmonton/Alberta/Canada
www. jennifersummerfeldt.com

Ordering Information:

Quantity sales. Special discounts are available on quantity purchases by corporations, associations, and others. For details, contact the "Special Sales Department" at the address above.

Jennifer Summerfeldt. --1st ed.

ISBN 978-1-9994972-2-4

This book is not for the faint of *heart.*

FOREWORD

Some years ago, when I was in my mid-fifties, I attended a family gathering and two of my twenty-something nieces came to me and said, '**Auntie you always look so put together. How do you do it?**'

My first reaction was a pleasant surprise since I had no idea that I appeared 'put together' to any member of a different generation. My next split-second reaction was that I had no answer to that question, yet I knew it demanded a genuine response.

I recognized in that moment I was being asked to share a response from my deepest place, from my *soul*.

So, I did what I usually do when I want to respond in the deepest way possible. I step back, get out of my own way, and listen to the words that come out of my mouth.

Here's what I heard myself say...

'Never be afraid to be lost. I've been lost many times and I've always been found. And each time I found my way, I became wiser and stronger, and more put together. So never be afraid to be lost.'

Did my twenty-something nieces hear me? Yes, and in the 30 seconds of silence that ensued before someone bumped us and brought us back to ordinary reality, we understood that in the right time we would each return to find the meaning in that moment of soul connection.

Initially, when I brought that answer up from my soul, I realized that I had never before articulated that I had been lost many times, and that being lost and then finding my way, was the catalyst for the greatest *transformations* in my life.

Over the years, and through many times, I have returned to that site of my greatest transformations - the *wasteland*.

The wasteland is real.

We are all called upon to cross it at some point in our lives. And, some wander aimlessly for years before finding their way out. Some never find it and spend a lifetime circling in the wilderness. Some get in and get out, reminding me of what Winston Churchill says: *'If you're going through hell, keep going'*.

And the pertinent thing about the wasteland is that no one can pull you out. Well-meaning folks can try, but they pull you out where you went in and you have to start over. Your loved ones can be waiting on the other side, but only you can find your way.

Reading this book, *Midwifery for the Soul*, has prompted me to revisit the wilderness and remember how being lost inspired my wholeness and alignment. In this book Jennifer offers new perspectives on pain, grief, chaos and ultimately transformation as we allow ourselves to enter the wasteland and become lost.

And, as with any journey of transformation, a map, a guide, a witness, a cheering section can be essential but it still comes down to the realization that **your act of will, and no other's, is the catalyst for lasting change.**

As the book unfolds, birth becomes the perfect blueprint for transformation. Rightly so, for how many women universally return to the knowing that birth and parenthood has changed them beyond imagination.

Birth is a wild place. A wilderness to cross, a mountain to climb, an ocean to tame. But nothing else brings a woman so close to moving from surrender to success than spanning the deepest cavern and creating Her *act of will*.

Read on as Jennifer creates more poetry of the Soul as women cross the Veils, flow with the Birthing Tides and invite the appearance of the Archangel.

There is mystical intelligence in these pages.

There is a cosmology unfolding.

There is hope and attunement and the story of a woman who has mastered the depths of her own soul.

And for those who want it, there is *Resurrection*.

Whapio Diane Bartlett
The Mother of The Matrona
www.TheMatrona.com

"But at last I understood from William Blake and Van Gogh and other great men, and from myself **- from the truth that is in me (and which I have at last learned to declare and stand up for, as I am trying to persuade you to stand up for your inner truth)-***at last I understood that writing was this: an impulse to share with other people, a feeling or truth that I myself had. Not to preach to them, but to give it to them if they cared to hear it. If they did not, fine; they did not need to listen. That was all right too. And I would never fall into those two extremes (both lies) of saying: "I have nothing to say and of no importance and have no gift"; or "The public doesn't want good stuff." When I learned all of this then I could write freely and jovially and not feel contracted and guilty and being such a conceited ass; and not feel driven to work by from resolution, by jaw-grinding ambition to succeed..."*
~ Brenda Ueland

TABLE OF CONTENTS

THE INVITATION

Come.
Walk with me if you dare
Into the interior landscape.
Let's call it soul
The world that exists behind the veil.

Inanna.
Peel back the skin
Layer upon layer.
As we expose the soul
Of your existence.

Ashes.
Nothing left, yet everything
Is alive in this terrain.
You know the place.

Knocking.
Ignored for some time now
Distracted by the world out here.
Excuse, after excuse
Exhausting.

Opening.
Down the channel
A birth canal.
Towards the light
Dar la luz.

Grey.
A whisper of a call
Dim upon entrance
Awaiting your return
Always.

Dance.
Upon the hills of pain
The tears of opening
The light of dawn
Is here.

And you ask.

What is soul?
'I don't know,' said the Mind.
'*I know*,' said the Soul.

Maybe it is all make-believe.
Then again, what isn't?

I don't *really* know how to write
grammatically speaking.
I know how to soul-speak.

Where rules are broken
The imaginal comes alive
Myth becomes reality
Reality becomes myth.

Aren't we just living
In a fairy tale anyway?

"How do you keep your heart open while in hell?"
Says my dear friend.

This is the quest, isn't it?

This book is an invitation to read these words with
an open heart, let them penetrate and take them
in, slowly, like sipping on a fine wine; it is meant
to be savoured in all its complexity. If no stirring
occurs, then let it go and move on. But know
that even a stirring of what some may consider
negative is a stirring of sorts, and carries with it a
message.

This message is for you, and only you.
I invite you to listen.

Listen to the nuances, the in-between, for the
clues that are woven throughout. There is a
knowing that is eternally available to you. This
knowing lives in the depth of your 'being'.

I call this place – the *soul*.

The ego speaks from analysis and criticism,
whereas the soul ponders and dwells.
I invite you to dwell upon these words.

We are about to go on a journey together, into the
underbelly of human suffering and trauma.

We are about to enter into soul territory.
This is not love and light; this is gritty and dark.
This is a landscape that is alive, well and ever
present. The womb of existence, full of watery
emotions and sensations.

No human has escaped trauma-land.

True, some of us are more acquainted with this
lived being that resides in our bodies. However,
being born earthbound is a promise of wrestling
with trauma.

Some call this human suffering.
Others call it the great curse.

Few risk to call it what it is – trauma-land.

Soul-writer Caroline Myss: 'If the path of
awakening is not for you, go back to the kitchen and
peel potatoes.'[1] In other words, stay asleep. We
are dormant for a reason, and until that veil is
lifted, we can stay naïve to the carnival we call
'life.'

Denial is contagious.

---

[1] Myss, C., Harvey, A. (2012). Divine Rebels: Saints, Mystics, Holy
     Change Agents, and You. Sounds True, Inc.

But for those of you who have seen behind the curtain of illusion, For those who know that there is a deep under current to our lived experiences, For those who know evil exists, To those who crave soul territory...

This book is for you.

Put on your seatbelts and be prepared for the unveiling of trauma-land. No niceties. No pretty lace. No curtailing. No spiritual bypassing. To awaken, to claim your soul, you must pass through this gate.

And for the few who have magically by-passed trauma-land, may you use your love and untethered soul for inspiring more love on this planet. And may you learn and listen from those who have had to find (and fight for) their light in the depths of darkness. May you continue to wake up to the soul that you are; you are not allowed to remain asleep.

If trauma is a major catalyst for spiritual awakening, and you have somehow managed to be protected from this beast, then I imagine you hold a special unique power that lies in the heart of hearts – use it wisely my friend.

I speak to and for those of us who have not been protected from trauma. I share a story, one of both lived experience and studious study, that begins to highlight this terrain. These words are coming directly from the soul to yours. As I unravel my own story, I also unravel the collected gifts of stories many have entrusted me with.

I am witnessing my own soul's quest as I lay down these words to integrate all that which has come and gone. I choose to share with you dear reader, a soul story which includes part journal, part poetry, and part ponder. And I hold hope that it inspires something within your being.

I have faced many deaths, and the one constant that has not perished in the chaos is my Soul's voice. Each time I come back to the familiar, which expresses itself with pen and paper.

Out of desire, generosity, and a will to be alive, I share with you my experiences, a blueprint and a framework that has greatly helped me navigate my own internal chaos. Without these sacred teachings (not from a text), I am not sure how I would have found my way through the dark night of the soul - an internal landscape of dank despair, debilitating pain and the quicksand of grief.

How does one speak to these matters – the experience of emergence out of dormancy and the slaying of the beasts within? How does one speak in a manner that ignites a familiar knowing within the other, in a way in which you can almost feel the living terrain and the magnificent power within?

I call this power – *Soul Force*.

The offering is one of hope. Hope that the sharing of my personal encounter with depression, melancholy, darkness, PTSD, despair and grief; and my courageous endurance and tenacity to find my way, will somehow inspire other Souls who are stricken with such pain.

You may be able to witness the transformation of the caterpillar to the butterfly. Yet you cannot *know* deep within your core what that experience was like for the butterfly. You can witness one or a thousand births and never know what that *felt* like for the mother. What I write about throughout these pages, is not an intellectual process, as it can only be known through experience alone.

Each labor is unique to a woman, and each soul birth (a journey of inner transformation) is unique to the individual.

Therefore, part of what I am weaving throughout these pages is what I consider to be a spiritual framework, inspired by my soul's quest using instinctual birth as a guiding metaphor. This birthing symbolism can assist with the navigation and understanding of your internal soul's experience with trauma, loss, pain, grief, and internal chaos.

In my experience, these sacred teachings about the cycle of life helped to inspire courage, determination, purpose, and a way through the immobilizing mess of grief, despair, and inner turmoil. The philosophy shared throughout these pages became the grace under fire that was so desperately needed. I speak about both my personal and perceptual experiences. As I was both the experiencer and the Witness to the experiences.

I learned to be the midwife of my own Soul's birth.

May I be so bold as to say that we all need to be midwifed in this holy way, and we all need to be the Midwife to our own Soul's awakening. I am honored that you have chosen to venture deeper into these murky waters and birthing tides. It is my deepest hope that in the end, you too will find the courage, faith, determination, and trust in this process of inner transformation.

The book is divided into two parts. The primary section is more recent musings that take you twisting and turning through the landscape of the gory and the glory. It is infused with soulful poetry and journal entries. It flows, but each section could be read on its own.

Take your time and read it as you would any creative poetic piece.

Part two guides you through the metaphor of instinctive birth as a transformative process. I chose to unpack the Holistic Stages of Labour and Birth, written and told by my wise and dear friend and mentor, Whapio Diane Bartlett. This paradigm of birth and midwifery has continued to be my guiding spiritual metaphor to understand human experiences of transformation and pain.

TERMINOLOGY

The System – This reference refers to the human body, including the mind, spirit, and soul. The system is the part of yourself that functions daily as you move through the world. It is fluid with life force and thrives when we are in harmony. The system is comprised of the brain, the nervous system and the energy system. Our system is encoded to thrive and survive. Learning how to work with your system in a healthy and optimal manner will provide you with the experience of grace and peace.

The Soul – From my point of view the term soul denotes the aspect of our 'self' that is energy in action. The soul is what we contact when we move our attention to the interior world, the landscape that exists in the realm of the imaginal. There are many players and parts in this territory that move us and animate us. The Soul, for some, is the part of our human experience that experiences it all. Non-linear, non-logical. Sacred and expansive. The soul is elusive in that we can only hypothesize about its existence. However, many agree upon the term and conclude that there is a 'soul'. One may also relate to it as consciousness, or awareness. Although we cannot deduce with certainty that the soul exists, I *sense* that it does. And I experience the soul as a creative life force moving itself to be expressed and known. Every time I fully embody an experience, I connect to the soul of being. For the purpose of this book, your experience of Soul is all that matters.

Trauma-Land – Denotes our human lived experience on earth, the notion that earth has been, and will continue to be, a playground full of chaos, destruction, pain, oppression, abuse, supremacy, and wounds. Seeing our lived experience through this lens is indeed challenging. However, the premise is to first accept what is and has been relentlessly unfolding for eons.

A Soul Wound – A psychological and/or physical wounding due to having endured something horrifying, terrifying, or deeply disturbing that fractures your connection with your soul.

A Collective Soul Wound – A generational wound that has not had the opportunity to heal. This wound lives in the psyche of your family, community, and environment. As such, due to epigenetics and cellular memory, you may *feel* the collective soul wound. Resulting in the need to heal not just your primary wound, but the collective wound.

The Mystery – That which is divine in nature, unknown to the human, rational mind, and consciousness. Part of the whole.

The Pain Body – Similar to soul wound, the pain body refers to the energetic imprint that is carried within your field – both physically and energetically. The pain body includes your genetic imprints, which would have been coded while in the uterus.

Consciousness – The part of 'you' that is aware that you are aware, that you are aware.

PART ONE
BACKWARDS & *Beginnings*

"[When] a trauma such as a disaster or major loss occurs and no parental help is available, there is no comforting or mirroring by a parent or other attachment figure. No systemic self-soothing or empathy is available internally or externally with any consistency. Chaos and instability follow. Dissociation or freezing occurs. This can lead to a sense of nothingness or emptiness"
~ Carol Forgash

DYING

Hallow sacred eyes
Decaying body
No more
No one.

Nothing matters anymore
But each moment
That arises in the
Moment, that it arises.

Death awaits
Calling your name.

If only you could surrender
Into the supportive
Embrace of death.

Agitated by the fight
To live for what?

I could see my eyes
My Fathers eyes
Looking back at me
In your eyes.

The tale I am about to share has its origin before I can remember. I know that some of the wailing and howling during those somber nights came from grief before time. There is no possible way that the amount of energy that came from my soul's cry was from this lifetime alone.

I thought back to my childhood to try to remember when I first noticed the gloomy constrictive, dark shadow that surrounded me. There were moments during my prime teen years that stood out as junctures in time that could have fed into my melancholy. Yet, it was before then that I was haunted with self-loathing, hatred, and despairing thoughts. Although I write from a place of embodiment and wholeness, as I mended together parts of my fractured soul, I can still sit in the muck of that voice.

Let's give that part a name – The voice of inner destruction. I know her well.

By the not so ripe old age of eleven, puberty presented itself as an initiating encounter with disgust and confusion of self, body, and being. Floating back even further I grasp at flashes during infancy and toddlerhood, with a sense of having been orphaned energetically, as my mother dealt with the death of my biological father. I am haunted by the image of having been passed around like popcorn, with no place or person to offer safe haven to rest within and upon. Craving a bosom that did not exist.

I asked my inner landscape, 'can I go back even further,' to a lineage of pain and hardship? And images of rape, burnings, brothels, queens and starvation lurked within my internal world. In particular, a scene appears like an impression within my mind's eye, and it is set within a date and time that my present I, cannot conceive of.

A woman in a barren kitchen; a large man slamming her around. Gruesome, the scene jumps, and he slices her throat because she spoke and spat in his face. She laid in his evil arms to die. Further back yet, fires and nooses float around in my field of awareness. Dangling feet. Grey images. Cold, distant and horrifying impressions of womanhood.

Today I find myself staring into the fires and imagine (remember) what it felt like to die in those flames. My sense of body dissolves, and it is as if I became one with the fire; my cells merging with all that surrounds, perhaps an ancient knowing about the dangers and liberation that can arise from the flames. Or just a dark twisted imagination.

Are these fabricated images, I ask myself?
Did I make them up,
Force them to the forefront?
Who really knows and who really cares?

How do we differentiate between imagination, magical thinking, and the imaginal realm? Jung calls the imaginal realm, *soul territory*.

I am told (I forget by whom) that unfinished grief can last lifetimes and when the soul finally releases it from that guttural place, although eventually being liberated, one can only feel overwhelmed by the torrent of energy moving through form. I experienced this notion as truth, as I let go of eons of pain gripped within the psyche of my cells.

I am sure you are starting to gather that this story, my living myth, a mere spec in the vastness of stories, is a tale of a woman's journey into the underworld; a battle with melancholy and darkness, debilitating despair, grief, and finally triumph.

This is my story, yet I know it is a shared collective story as well. It is colorful, graphic, and at times, even bland. I can be bored by the pain, if that is even possible, tired of the dramatic tales from the human battlefields. And, when the words cannot describe what is being experienced, I paint. I write. I create. I use painting as a form of expression to bring to life what dwells within this internal landscape. Not the kind of painting one would want to purchase; this is soul painting. It is ugly, yet, profoundly beautiful in its dreadfulness.

I do not think that my life was/is different than anyone else's. I never valued my historical stories as having meaning, nor did I pause to integrate any of my life experiences. I was always too busy overcoming obstacles and striving for greater achievement, which acted as a good distraction from *feeling* anything real.

My most desired achievement was to be able to say to my family, "Yes, I am (finally) happy."

At every turn in the road I believed I was perpetually failing because I could not answer that one question: 'Are you happy?' with absolute certainty. Eventually, that question became the measure of a good life and a good person. But I did not know if I was ever going to touch that place – happiness. I knew that I was dissatisfied, but I did not *know* what 'dissatisfied' really *felt* like. I just knew that for my entire life something felt 'off.' This has become my barometer now, and I can say with certainty when something feels *off*. And I know now that I'd better damn well pay attention!

Terrified that I might one day be labeled as a depressive person, due to the stigma within my maternal family, I did everything to avoid the topic of conversation around 'happiness'. All the while, silently paranoid that this haunting state of melancholy was in actuality, my core essence (unchangeable). I developed an ability to sense (intuit) at a young age, yet had little understanding about this heightened empathetic response. I found myself surrounded by plastic faces and emotions, confused by these disconnected states.

Rarely did people present themselves as *real* to
me; I could only know this in hindsight. I had not
yet developed any skills to be able to speak to this
dissonance that I perceived, nor could I honor
my *knowing* as truth. How could I? I was merely
a child. All of which led to an internal belief that
I was the *crazy* one and all the others were *sane*.
Eventually, I imploded in on myself, resulting in my
silence – it was not safe to speak my truth. I never
fully understood what I was actually sensing. But I
knew I was experiencing something.

Throughout the years, I prided myself with the
fact that I did not cry – not when I broke bones,
sprained ankles, got into fights, or when family
members died. I perceived this as a sign of
strength, power and control. If I did not show
tears, then no one could label me as depressive
and I would not *feel* the pain – even though I live
with a very sensitive relational heart. I could
endure the pain of the body and mind, yet the pain
of the heart was too much for me. I had learned
how to turn off the valve.

I had stopped the flow of heart-juice. I'd had to.
And it kept me safe for some time.

However, I learned that you can only keep the gate
closed for so long. Eventually, there comes a time
in life when you lose your footing, when life as you
knew it crumbles beneath your feet. Some may
say this is the great catalyst, necessary for change

and growth. Many, including myself, will keep these catalysts at a distance, continuing to power through with an illusion that somehow you have control over your life. As if!

In time, however, the tornado begins, chaos reigns, and you get swept up in with the flying debris.

This is what I call: *The great collapse.*

You will know when this time has come. Some will pride themselves in being able to keep their shit together when everything is 'falling apart'. Yet, eventually you too must fall apart in order for deep transformation to occur.

I call this time - when you avoid letting the tornado whirl you into a new kind of insanity - *a holding pattern.*

You know you must land, but you cannot find safe landing, so you circle and circle like an airplane. Eventually, you will run out of stamina and your system comes crashing down. You know the scene: you are diagnosed with an illness; someone close dies; you lose your job; you lose your identity; you lose your community; a relationship ends; something tragic happens.

Either way, you must come down in order to survive. For some, like myself, you can keep yourself in a holding pattern for years (some might say a lifetime).

As expected, my whole system eventually crash-landed. No longer being able to bear the weight of the external pressure, stress, and chaos, I lost my footing in what I knew to be the *real* world. I watched life go by, all the while my system collapsing. Many external circumstances caused this expected collapse, which later (much later) lead to a diagnosis of Post-Traumatic Stress Disorder (PTSD). PTSD is the language we can understand. We can see symptoms, and with symptoms we can attempt to create treatment plans. Even naming it as such – PTSD – keeps *it* at a distance.

Clinging to hope that PTSD will not swallow me whole, I ravenously attempted to fix the *problem* outside of myself, trying to learn about it, understand it, change it and make it go away. But all the while my brain was deteriorating in function at a rapid rate. And I was convinced that I was losing my mind and my intelligence.

I had lost control of my faculties – emotions, thoughts, mental images, behaviours. It was as if I was possessed. My only way out, I imagined, was to saw or blow off my head. *The head was my problem.* If only I could get out of my head, or get rid of my head. The ultimate dismemberment, from head and heart. Take it off at the throat was the image. Gory and all.

This felt so real.

I believed that it was *me* having those images and thoughts. I believed 'I' was therefore defective. Broken. Gone. How does one return from this place?

I was forced to face what I believed to be a great failure and sign of weakness - seeking professional support. Remember: I was terrified of being seen as melancholic, but what I was experiencing was worse than melancholy. My entire being and system felt as if I'd hijacked by an intruder. I had lost control, allowing myself to receive a diagnosis and surrender to the fact that along the healing path, external support was needed, was part of my healing journey. As humans, we are not intended to heal alone, and yet my shame ran so deep, I had convinced myself that I must do it all alone.

I had no trust in humans; I had no trust in life itself.

I have since spent many years questioning what it means to heal and feel wholeness. As I write, I am still in the process of *becoming*. Albeit, I am millions of miles away from the 'voice of inner destruction'. That part is quiet. Maybe even gone, if that is even possible? It is hard to believe that there was a time, not too long ago, in which I actually thought, with all my might, that the only way out was to dismember my head. I knew *something* had to die, for *something* to be born. Thankfully, the death that followed was that of the ego-death. I kept my finger away from the trigger for the sake of my children. But during those dark despairing nights, the notion gave me great comfort. To end life as we know it.

Face to face with my dark night of the soul, I had a choice: Dare to enter, or choose the ultimate escape. I chose to enter the barren lands of my *soul-scape*. And with that, I was swept down to learn how to navigate those waters. Soul territory does not come with a map; I had to find the map that would help to guide this inner terrain. *They* say we all have an inner compass, and I was desperate to find mine. I anchored myself in the fact that my three living children needed me; they needed me to be *alive*. No matter how rough the waters were (and as you will read, they were rough at times) I never stopped searching for this *inner compass*. Healing is a process of integration, so that the soul can awaken to itself and be known; to be conscious that *it* exists.

DEATH.

Born into death.
Imprinted by death.
Haunted by death.
Death
Always at the door.
Afraid to breath.
She may come for me.

What is the purpose of life
if death awaits us all?
What is the purpose of healing
if death still awaits?
What is the purpose of working
if death eventually catches up?

We live.
We die.

Some of us never live,
Never take that breath
                of trust.
Never allow the soul
                to be born.
Frozen in fear
            waiting.

Death is familiar
                living is not.

Comforted to remain asleep
Then to open one's soul eyes.

What does it mean to choose life?

I am afraid to live.
To arrive.
To land.
To root.

What is the purpose,
if death awaits my return?

Trauma AS THE INITIATOR FOR SPIRITUAL ACTIVISM

---

*"There is a descent to a state of death in life. We look and feel dead, **but something is happening under the skin**-if we let it. The mask of the old self is dying-harbinger of resurrection...The dark, enclosed place of the cocoon is necessary for metamorphosis to complete itself" ~ Miriam Greenspan.*

TRAUMA-LAND

Hands
Getting dirty
Moss blood
Bowels of The Mother
Complexity of layers
Beauty in the mess
Pieces
Like pealing
Lotus flower.

To unpack the heavy nature of the topic of trauma, one needs to tread with reverence. To enter the territory of trauma, deep within the soul, requires a humble entry. These days 'trauma-informed care' is flung around as tag lines all over the place. On one hand this is good – we are waking up to the notion that unresolved trauma is at the root of it all. On the other hand, the ways in which we are engaging in the conversation is still within arm's reach.

Trauma is over there and happens to 'those' people. And I am over here, untouched by trauma.

This gap is at the core of our suffering. This gap prevents you and me from knowing our soul. This gap prevents us from connecting, truly connecting, with others. This gap keeps us in isolation and keeps us in magical thinking. The dream that somehow, somewhere, at some time, trauma did not impact you (me). That in some way, we were saved from the suffering that many 'others' have to endure.

We escaped *trauma-land*.

I want to preface this with an assumption. The assumption is that no one has escaped trauma. I know that I wrote about this perception in the introduction: That perhaps few people have. But as we delicately explore the *body* of trauma, I posit that no one has escaped trauma-land.

Trauma is the lived experience of humans; it is part of our journey. Part of what journey, you may ask? The journey of awakening to that which resides at the core of your being – your soul.

And in that, is your *liberation*.

I wish it was different. I question myself often about this perception. I question my beliefs and ask myself: is this just my tainted viewpoint? Am I making this up? Do others perceive the world out there differently – without trauma-land being real? Of course, we all have different perceptions of reality. Of course, we all come to our own conclusions about our experiences.

Thus, this is merely my reality based on my astute observations. However, I do want to point out a few facts that I think we can all agree upon.

We are living in the era of massive environmental disaster that is alive and obvious;
We are living in times of great wars (when has there not been war?);
We see huge gaps between extreme wealth and poverty;
We experience political leaders who are cruel, racist, and narcissistic to the extreme;
We *know* that global warming is happening and that it is having a detrimental impact on the earth's health;
We continue to witness racism and oppression;

Slavery is still alive and reinstated with a new term
– institutionalized prison;
We are aware of the all the horrible acts that
thousands have facilitated in the name of their
God;
We are aware of the devastation that colonization
has had on our First Nations people;
We are still living in a child abuse crisis;
Children are still being sexually abused;
Women are still being raped;
Men are still being raped;
Teenagers are still bullying each other;
Suicide is higher than ever;
Addictions are still devastating families;
Prozac is on the rise along with every other
psychopharmaceutical being pushed by the
companies for profit;
Mental illness is still that 'thing' that so many
are afraid of – even if we have mental awareness
month;
Elderly abuse is coming out of the closet;
We are trapped in the worldview that
consumption at all cost is what we live for;
We are suffering from disease and obesity at high
rates;
Food security is a real concern;
Water security is a real concern;
Deforestation is a real concern;
Air quality is a real concern;
Human trafficking is a real concern;

Human collateral for Western consumerism is a
real concern;
And we are plugged into our devices practically 24
hrs a day.

I can keep finding more examples to support the
notion that since humans have lived on earth, life
has been a minefield full of trauma. And the truth is
that no one, not even me, wants to believe that this
could be true; That we are born into a shitshow.
Cognitive dissonance is one of the ways we cope
and search to find all the opposite 'truths' for what
I just listed. To ease the heart, we would prefer to
focus on the Light – The good in our world.

Of course, there is good. We live in duality,
both light and dark exist in this plane of reality.
However, what I am proposing is that we cannot
just live in the good if we want to call our Spirit
home and claim our soul. We have to go down
and under before we can come up and out. No
doubt there is a force that is far greater than
the pain of human existence. The key is to not be
swallowed by the doom and gloom of our personal
and collective experiences, simultaneously, to
not detach and dissociate. The path is about
embodying all that is – the light and the dark.
Being able to hold the tension of both light and
dark, pain and love, within your interior world. And
the soul can do this – It is time to touch *home.*

The other night, I engaged in a tantalizing conversation, influenced by fine cocktails, deep in the wounds and nestled between the mountains. Naked we sat together, my women friends and I, soaking up the smell of cedarwood in the heat of a handcrafted hot tub. We nattered about this very topic – the tension between pain and love, good and bad, light and dark, trauma and bliss. As we each explored my suggestion that as humans, we live in 'trauma-land'.

Immediately you could feel the resistance to the preposterous statement I'd just declared. As I unpacked it further, sharing that to accept this perspective did not mean I'm endorsing living in 'the wound', we all relaxed into the possibility of this being a truth. The fear, of course, being that if we agreed that trauma is everywhere, then a bubbling sense of despair and hopelessness would rise to the surface. Suffocating even the most optimistic person.

But what if we could allow the senses to relax into this possibility without needing to do anything about it – not yet anyways.

Begin to scan your interior world, your lifespan, your family lifespan for generations. Has it ever been without trauma? And, if it is too close to home to scan your lifespan, go ahead and look outside of you. Float through environmental, political, racial, and civic catastrophes. Would you agree that there is a current throughout time as we know it that is full of trauma?

And yet, **trauma does not have to identify you.**

This is indeed the catcher. Before we can even begin to peel back this notion, before we can understand within our cells what it means to not be identified with trauma, we must first accept its constant presence. I had to do just this. Initially, when I dove into the studies of trauma theory, now known as traumatology, I was hopeful (and I still am, just on a different level), I was hopeful that I could heal from trauma and that I could help others heal. I was not aware that under my hope, was a profound insecurity.

Fear. Fear based on a concept that trauma is bad and needs to be eradicated. I had a grandiose perception of myself that somehow, I could contribute to this dream to alleviate human suffering. If only I could hold and help enough people, we would free ourselves from the impact of trauma. We could be free from suffering.

A belief: to get *rid* of trauma is the *ultimate* goal.

If you are anything like me, and have permeable skin – feel everything – then this goal is deadly. It brought me into the underworld, fast. The more I showed up in service with the intention to 'eradicate trauma', the more ill I became. I remember with such clarity the experience of floating in the field of trauma as I sought to understand its root. This brought me soul-soul with the nature of evil.

When we start dismantling, or attempting to dismantle evil, we are bound to find ourselves sucked into a dark abyss of soul. My mind yearned to understand why evil existed in the first place. Further, why on earth would our human form be thrown into a field of trauma?

It seemed like a sick cosmic joke – or a grueling training of sorts. Training for what?

The deeper I went in, the more I could soul-see the mess we are in. And the more disempowered I felt to do anything about it. Seriously, I am just a spec. One cell in a huge sea of cells. What could I possibly do to lift the veil on trauma? Sure, learning about the nervous system and how it stores trauma is empowering and insightful. However, restoring our nervous system back to health and coherence is not the end result. There is more. A healthy nervous system helps you go deeper, and that depth is the territory of the Soul.

The quest, as I have come to know it, is to liberate oneself from the cords of trauma so to release the soul from the wheel of suffering. However, let us not forget that unprocessed trauma devastates and impoverishes the soul. Few consciously choose to dive into this vast landscape; and few know how to navigate their interior world. Truly, a world unto itself.

To speak about trauma, we must first enter the *womb*.

If you are here, on this earth, your primary environment was that of the dark womb. The world of water and sound. You were breathed into form. The spacious buoyancy and swooshing of the great Mothers' waters; **The sacred home of stillness –** The womb.

So much is happening during womb time. This 'meat-suit' (as one of my brave client's stated) is going through a patterned biological response to cellular division and growth. The pattern of human form magically unveils within the waters of the womb. And as this journey of form takes place, where are *you* during the process? Are you the cells dividing? The embryo? The developing fetus? Are you conscious? Are you known? Where is your consciousness in relationship to this developing embryo?

Come with me for a moment and begin to re-imagine yourself in your mother's womb. Imagine all those biological processes occurring to form what you relate to as 'you'. As this process is taking place, at what point did you become a 'you'? How much control did you have over this process of incubation? The answer is none. If *you* are not in control of this process, who or what is? What is behind the magic of our biological blueprint?

There are differing perspectives on this notion. One is from a materialistic and reductionistic point of view, which voices that there is no consciousness outside of the physical body. Therefore, when the brain is online, consciousness exists. And when the brain circuit dies, so does consciousness, along with any sense of 'self'. In essence, there is no evidence for 'life after death'; no consciousness after death of the physical. Let us call this point of view: materialistic and mechanistic.

The second point of view, which is more widely adopted especially amongst religious organizations and beliefs, is that of the physical being separate from consciousness – the physical form houses consciousness. And some believe that the *body* is conscious at the onset of conception, while others argue that consciousness is 'alive' around 49 days after conception, when the pineal gland is developed during the embryonic phase. It is curious to note that the pineal gland is considered to be the 'spiritual gland' because it produces a hormone called DMT; which is said to be involved with expanded states of consciousness.

A third perspective to ponder is that consciousness is always present, that there is no end or beginning, that there just is. And consciousness is in relationship to the physical, soon to become the house it will inhabit for a while. One can argue that from this angle, consciousness is not personally attached to the vehicle it houses. However, perhaps through the laws of electro-magnetism, for whatever reason, consciousness finds its way to the spark of creation and conception. And that initial spark of light – which literally occurs when the sperm penetrates the ovum – draws towards it, consciousness.

Consciousness is not personality; nor sense of self. Consciousness just *is* present to the unfolding, without attachment. And throughout the process of conception, embryonic development, fetal development and birth, one thing we all seem to agree upon is that the alive baby becomes animated with the inhalation of its first breath.

I will ask the question again: where were you during this heroic journey of conception and birth? Were you witnessing it? Were you present to what was unfolding? Were you in the background? Were you merely your brain in development? Most spiritual traditions speak to the notion that we are born asleep; albeit we appear awake. For what reason would we be born asleep?

You are painting the painting that has never been painted
before. Creating an art form that has never been seen
before.
~ Said my Friend

When Insecurities Win

On the edge of dreams coming true
A manifestation of love
A passion for change,
Lasting change.

All that once was, washed away
As the raindrops continue to fall,
Falling into the unknown.

Painting a painting
that has never been painted before
Creating an art form
that has never been seen before,
Says a dear friend.

Reminding me to stay open
During times of vulnerability
When insecurities always win.

No doubt, this is a hard road to travel – the road to *home*. There are nights when you feel like death is upon you; you feel it whispering from behind, like a nagging mosquito. As you explore your interior landscape, there are moments where the pain within is so great that you feel as if you're breaking open.

Heart pried wide open by life's crowbar; there is nothing comfortable about this.

Many get lost in the pain, spiraling deeper into the torment of despair, unsure where to go or how to handle the intensity of the experience. Few know how to navigate the labor pains of their life; rather they escape and numb themselves. In this numb state, there are moments of relief – a break.

Yet, when they crash down again (inevitably so) they are struck by the beating stick. Reminded that this intensity has no escape; *the only way is through*. Fuck the 'going through,' thinks the mind. In the flailing of the pain, the soul-pain, many perpetuate painful actions. Cultivating more pain in the process; whipping themselves with their own Willow switch. Many find themselves in dramatic circumstances with life slapping them in the face everywhere they turn.

Is this the cruel joke, this 'human' thing?

Then the cycle begins again, escaping the pain with addictions, drugs, alcohol, sex, work, T.V. etc. In this, they may experience moments of relief, and then more pain courses through their marrow – yours and my marrow.

There is no healing in this cycle of pain and abuse, there is only 'getting by.' The weight is so heavy to bear. It is fantasy to believe that numbing and denial offer any relief; rather it functions as a distraction from the inner work that is calling your attention.

Pause for a moment. I am sure you are thinking to yourself: How dare you, or anyone, tell me that I am somehow perpetuating this cycle of pain. Some of us entertain the new age philosophy that denotes 'we are responsible for what we create or attract'. I don't know about you, but I sure went down the rabbit hole of this one, especially when The Secret came to screen.

I remember thinking to myself, if this is true, how can so many humans suffer tragic circumstances. It is akin to blaming the victim. And something in my body sensed that this was wrong. However, I never stopped exploring this point of view. How can I know the concept to be true without going down the human blame train? I had to dig deeper and not take the notion – we create our reality – at face value. It requires an expanded state of awareness to grasp its complexity. Similar to reading any spiritual or mystical text, it is not intended to be understood from a linear personality thinking mind.

This reminds me of women in labor who are trapped in their minds.

Fixated on the pain in hope of controlling the process, yet afraid to go deeper into the intensity of the labor. They can manage the pain from this place, so they remain at 4 cm for hours or days, in the end, exhausting their stamina. Women who find themselves stuck at this stage often need a catalyst in order for them to open more deeply into the process.

The catalyst may be an anger release, tears, talking about fears, or speaking some deep secret. Although often we are told that things are not progressing because of the baby's position, rarely, is it position alone. Usually it is a dance between intensity, the unknown, and the primal power and fear of bringing forth life.

At this stage of labor, the woman has not yet crossed through the veil, she is walking on the edge, hanging on to what she once knew and is afraid to move forward into the unknown territory of being blown wide open – physically and metaphysically.

This razor edge I speak of is one that you must go over in order to encounter the depths of your journey; the depths of your soul. You know you are at this edge when you can feel an inner stirring, and yet the pain is still manageable. You manage to control the intensity of the pain and keep it at bay via distractions. You believe you are doing well and that this is all you need to endure. However, this is not the case.

Welcome the holding pattern. The place in which you remain stuck in a cycle of malaise and mediocrity – life's 4 cm. At this stage of the decent, there is a familiar comfort. Like the mother who finds comfort and a sense of accomplishment knowing that she is managing labor so well – at only 4 cm of dilation. Clearly, there is still a huge journey ahead.

Why go deeper and plunge into the abyss of the unknown, you might ask? For what purpose would we invite in Inanna's decent?

As with the laboring mother who remains at this stage, she cannot birth from this plane of reality, she must go deeper into the experience and let the waves of contractions take her further away from a reality once known. As she does, you too will exhaust yourself in managing the pain from the holding pattern, by dancing on the edge.

A mother cannot dance here for days before exhausting herself. Usually, medical intervention is necessary after little progression and hours and days of being in-between worlds. With no change in sight, some intervene within 24 hours and others could be days; inevitably intervention is the outcome.

The problem with our technocratic society is that we intervene mechanically (drugs and machines) rather than, soulfully and energetically, far too often. Staying with the metaphor of birth, when external intervention happens, a woman senses a loss of power. She perceives that she was robbed of an opportunity to find her way through. Far too often this is internalized, and the mother identifies herself and her birth as a failure.

It is important to interject here and make known that I am not implying that every mother should birth without intervention or instinctively. I have been around the culture of birth for far too long to hold that naïve belief anymore (albeit once I did). It is however within our birthright to have access to that potential and opportunity. As well, fact would have it that far too often women feel devastated by their birthing experience or at the very least, numb or indifferent.

Often, I found that a loving presence asking the 'right' questions, encourages you to face your fears and to create an environment that is dark, warm, safe, trusting, nurturing, and free from distractions, is helpful at the immovable phase. Usually, when a woman is stuck in her labor, it is because she is thinking her way through the labor. As already mentioned, labor cannot progress when preoccupied by the rational brain. Think about it - she is about to bring forth life, earth bound, and somehow it would be a good time to use our thinking, rational brain?

There is nothing rational about giving birth; and nothing rational about healing.

Pain causes you to enter an altered state, on purpose, and it is calling your attention for a reason. Sometimes the reason is a warning, a legitimate response to danger and harm. However, the pain I am referring to is what I would call *purposeful pain.*

Labour is purposeful pain – to birth.
Grief is purposeful pain – to cleanse the heart.
Injury is purposeful pain – to warn.
Sickness is purposeful pain – to surrender.

There is a message in the pain and rather than fight it, what would happen if you surrendered to it? Why not just plunge into it with a 'fuck it' mentality and take the pain head on? You might surprise yourself, because with this focused determination and courageous attention, the pain shifts.

The shifting of pain is magical, and it stores information that can guide the way. If we listen. Birth is a very mystical experience and yet, very real and physiological. When you fight the pain and resist it, you will experience more pain. I say mystical because a woman gives birth from an altered state of consciousness. Her sense of self has been obliterated just before she brings forth the light. It is mystical because there is an ego death that occurs during labour and birth. Similar to psychedelic ego-deaths and long-term meditating ego deaths. These transcendental experiences initiate this death.

Unfortunately, we forget to include 'ego-death' during childbirth classes. Someone who chooses a psychedelic experience is most likely saying yes to the pain of the ego-death. However, not every pregnant woman wants to sign up for an ego-death in labour. Is it any wonder that for many, childbirth is excruciatingly hard? It is hard for a reason. The woman is being initiated into motherhood.

Thus, we have learned to equate pain with danger and ultimately death – physical or mental. Hence, we will fight against it with all our might, attempting to control every aspect in hopes to alleviate suffering. The irony is that more suffering is endured along this route.

Courage is the choice to move forward, even though there may be fear and pain. Courage is action with an open heart. There must be a motivating purpose to continue forward to experience some of the most challenging emotions: grief, fear, despair, anger. Of course, with labour, the motivation is obvious – to receive a child. However, the motivation to wake up from our dormancy and move through the dungeon of despair is not so obvious.

As previously mentioned, I am challenged by the new age information that encourages us to think differently; the notion that thought is creating our reality. I have struggled with this concept for many years, reprogramming my beliefs and listening closely to what limits my life experience. Although, the power of thought absolutely *does* alter your perception of reality, it is not enough to just change the thought pattern. If the emotional material remains frozen in your system, no amount of 'positive self-talk' will remedy it. The action of experiencing the pain will shift your internal world. The catcher is that you must be able to hold the pain in conscious awareness so as not to be swallowed by it. Every time you pop out of conscious awareness, separating your awareness with the pain, you get thrown back in to try again.

It reminds me of a bad dream I had not too long ago. The dream was always about intruders breaking into my home (my safe haven) and nothing I do could stop them. I was not strong enough to hold the door closed, and I had lost the ability to scream. My force alone was unwavering, but the intruders always 'won' – they gained forced entrance into my dwelling. I am always overwhelmed with terror when this dream occurs.

My emotional body is fused with the experience and every cell in my body believes that is happening to me. I feel trapped and out of control. And my impending death is looming over me.

Lately, I have been trying to 'wake up' in the dream. It occurred to me that the trick is to float above the scene, to remember that consciousness can witness what is happening, but it is not being harmed by it. I am attempting to hold equilibrium within my emotional body, as the intruders attempt to enter, so that I am not drowning in panic. This idea of holding equilibrium staying with what is happening without becoming destabilized by the emotional experience–is the precious *golden spot*.

Liberation and ultimate freedom occur in these moments of homeostasis. That said, few of us were taught how stabilize our nervous systems when activated, or how to *be with* our emotions without succumbing to the chemical disaster that explodes within our system.

That said, once this internal landscape has shifted, your mental chatter lessens and aligns with your soul. How you navigate the pain, *is within your control* – and this is where the notion of choice lies.

Even though I was poo-pooing the new age philosophy, it is true that the thoughts associated with the pain indeed intensify or diminish the experience.

However, thought alone is not enough to shift your internal reality. Thought *plus the will* and determination to take different actions will indeed cause an effect, in return, changing your reality as you know it. There is a place deep within, that wants to be living a soul-expressed life, in harmony with the mind and heart. This 'place', this knowing, will continue to knock at your inner eye until you wake the fuck up. Soul is not always nice; however, it is bathed in love.

When I choose to consciously step out of my cycle of chaos and pain, after many years of enduring much drama, abuse, neglect, frustration, pain, depression, and chaos; I did so with all of my power and intention. I set out to battle my inner demons with a vengeance. I assumed that everyone wants to do this. I was mistaken in this assumption; most humans prefer distraction and denial as their form of an expressed life.

For myself, it was a conscious choice motivated by a 'fuck it' mentality. In deep contemplation and despair, I had *had* enough. It dawned on me that there was indeed an impact from my life choices and chaos. This impact affected not only me, but also my closest circle of influence; my family and dear friends. Up until this point I was operating out of my programs. Those programs that are casted in utero; trapped in the vulnerable net of intergenerational traumas. Born into this veil, which in turn, becomes the lens through which you/I experience our world.

It is important to note that choice is not available to everyone. For many we live in reaction. Reaction to our life in constant struggle for survival. Reaction is not choice. Reaction to our circumstances is instinctive – motivated by our cerebellum (reptilian brain) to keep us alive. It is very hard to make conscious choice from reactionary living. Hence why, the primary motivation in this state needs to be safety. If the external environment is literally unsafe – abuse, poverty, neglect – the nervous system will have a difficult time unplugging from its survival circuits. The first act of conscious choice, under these circumstances, is to seek out safety and support.

I had removed myself from my unsafe toxic environment and therefore I could now consciously decide, with much effort, that I would no longer choose to bring chaos into my life because I could not bear to witness the impact that it was having on those who love me. In particular, my children.

I was starting to wake the fuck up.

It was the feeling and energy of love, which stimulated a feeling of worthiness, for the first time in a long while. I saw the ripple effect that my choices had on others and the world around me. I knew, deeply in my core, that I was not alone; that I am interconnected and that the law of cause and effect is indeed a Truth.

It was from this place of internal power, that I began to call my Spirit back and immediately made significantly different choices.

It is this quality of thought, connected with action and a deep sense of love, which sets a different reality into motion. Once this energy is moving, it must be released and felt. Women in labor are encouraged to feel and move and vocalize – breath moves the energy of pain. The labour pain of my soul taking form sounded like deep ancient wails that filled my bathtub each night. Coming into contact with this inner power meant dissolving all that I once knew.

Remaining quiet is not an option. Women in labour are encouraged to open their mouths, loosen their jaws and ROAR with all the power of the universe to bring forth life (when they are supported in the right ways). Finding your primal voice and letting the wild-self moan, groan, and scream is part of the process of awakening to that which has been dormant. This must come from the depths within, and we all carry this place of power.

Sounds from the throat differ greatly from sound that comes from the belly of the earth.

Again, the central imperative is to stand buoyant within this storm, as you midwife your own soul birth. There is no sound too great to frighten. A spiritual midwife knows this terrain, knows the power of birth, knows the voice of the underworld, and knows the roars of a primal voice. She never wavers in this trust; and as you become undone and find your voice, you hang on to this buoy in the water for comfort and grace.

Remember that the only way through the chaos, is to go deeper within.

Many are detached from this primal voice or the core power that we all possess. Who has been your role model? How are you to learn about that soul voice and power within? In primal birthing, women find this strength and it forever changes them – I know because I have witnessed this to be true. When left alone in birth, undisturbed and deeply trusted, they explore this power and eventually roar their baby from womb to world.

Women who have done this carry a secret about the world of transformation; yet many women are silenced, and this kind of power is hidden. How are we to learn, if we can never see or hear these stories?

Often, we only hear the stories of chaos and pain, rarely the stories of triumph and transformation.

Discombobulated

I'm floating – day and night.
I feel like I'm moving through water
like my spirit is outside of my body
moving alongside my body
but not a part of my body.

Split.
Dissociated.
Exhausted.

Spiritually, exhausted.
I'm fine when I am with the sensations
as long as I don't have to engage with the world.

I have a metallic taste in my mouth
like electricity running through me.
I've tasted something like this before.

Worried my life force is dwindling
As I lose stamina.
I'd like to know what is happening
I know it's not physical
It *is* spiritual energy.

My cells are physically morphing
Dissolving
Discombobulated
Distorted

I no longer recognize,
Me.

A Vision

A deeply profound, meditative experience that occurred during part of my healing journey is worth sharing at this point. Although there have been many, what some would call shamanic visions, this particular impression stood out. The image was powerful and vivid. It was as if I was watching a movie and I was the main character. I was separate from this image and yet, I could *feel* the scene. I find it hard to share these personal experiences, because I am afraid that the power and magic will be diminished in the sharing. Yet, the imagery was so inspiring that I feel compelled to speak of it.

What I saw, was a passage; a journey of the underworld. I watched as the character descended into an abyss. The descent was intense, like Alice falling down the rabbit hole. It felt like a tube of sorts and was dark, black dark. I felt fear, terror, and panic pound throughout my system as I sensed my way through this somber tunnel. I experienced objects grabbing at me, tearing my clothes off and scratching my skin until I bled.

The pain was horrific. I felt cold, naked, and chaotic. I was sucked into a void of sorts, and my life's chaos was the catalyst that pushed me over this edge. All this felt so real and visceral as I experienced the great fall – what I have later termed as the ego's fall.

Eventually, I hit *a* bottom.

This was indeed foreign ground. It was still dark, so dark, the kind of darkness that creeps you to the core. You open your eyes and yet you see nothing, so you keep them closed even in the obscure hole. All I could do was trust, blinded by the darkness, as I faced the paralyzing fear. I had no choice but to move through the thick cavern like terrain. I noticed, or it occurred to me, that grief was the catalyst that kept moving me. All of my senses were activated, and I continued to feel the dampness, the coldness, and the dankness.

This *was* the channel of despair.

I was alone yet surrounded by others wailing here. They were stuck in this state, tormented by the chaos and pain of misery. I experienced myself spinning in circles and feeling like I was being sucked under further. At times, it felt like quicksand. There was no fast way out of this desolate underworld, and it manufactured my deepest fears.

Keeping my external eyes closed and working to open my inner eye, I let the psychic pain carry me away. What I observed was that the more I let go and flowed with the pain, resisting nothing and surrendering to it all, I was propelled forward. At times, it felt like walking through molasses; sticky, dark, slow, and thick. This was a heavy, weighted state of being.

I understood, because I was shown that many get stuck in the whirlwind of despair, creating more chaos and cycling like a tornado. It was conveyed that during this phase some choose death – unable to see and trust that there is a way through. As I watched myself struggle, I felt enormous compassion arise within my Being. Not just for me, but for all those who struggle during this phase.

As with labor, there is a time to be with others but there is part of the journey that must be completed alone. This was the 'alone time' along my journey. I was keenly watching during this vision as I saw and felt the weight begin to lift. A speck of light, grey like, casting a shadow at the end of the tunnel of despair. Approaching this shadow, I could see that there was a ledge that I had to climb up to pull myself out of this pit.

As I attempted to elevate myself up onto this landing, hands were grabbing and tugging at me with full force. It was as if chaos was trying to suck me back into the tunnel of despair. Yet, something was alive in me. A powerful core took charge and pulled me over the ledge – in the way that swimmers pull themselves out of the water, just much higher.

The howling voices in the background never stopped, but I was buffered by the ledge. All alone, collapsed on this cement-like grounding. At this phase, I was acquainted with great rest. A glorious moment of relief and repose, during which time, I curled up into a fetal ball and wept tears of relief and exhaustion.

There are few words to describe the kind of soul exhaustion at this point.

The laborious journey thus far had called upon all of my endurance, strength, and stamina. As I observed myself weep, I knew I had not completed my quest and that there was still work to be done. Part of me wanted to lay there forever, wishing that the 'grey zone' was it – had I arrived? However, the grayness and quietude informed me that I was not yet through.

Gathering another layer of courage, endurance, and determination to move forward, I peered onward and up. And in the horizon for the first time, I saw a brilliant light. At this stage of the *meditation* I thought to myself: *This cannot be true.* But my Soul knew that it was the Light that will guide the way through. Eager to leave the tunnel of despair behind me, the rest of the journey was an upward climb. I was surrounded by a nature-filled, cave-like tube, clean with the brilliance of the glow of the Light. It continued to get brighter along the way.

There I was, ragged and dragging one foot in front of the other at a snail's pace. I knew that I was starting the ascension phase of the healing journey. It felt very different in this new cylinder-like environment than the tunnel of despair. And far more hopeful than the grey quiescence. I had an inner drive that was motivating me. A heart full of desire, appreciation, grace, humility, and faith (not religious faith, raw faith of moving forward towards the unknown).

I was told by a distant voice: *"Along this remaining healing path, you will be needing assistance. Ask for it, for you no longer need to endure this terrain alone. Recover, rebuild, and replenish for you will need the strength near the end."*

Upon which I *awoke.*

I have kept that nugget of gold in my back pocket as I continued along my path to find my way through the dark night of the soul. Always remembering the golden light that I saw, trusting in the process, and finding the support along the way.

To Grieve

Do not celebrate my life,
When I die.

I want you to grieve.
Grieve so deeply that your heart explodes open.

I want you to wail;
Wail a love song.

Fall to your knees in heartache
And call out my name.

Do not pretend you are okay
When in reality you are
     Breaking
      Open.

If you cannot grieve
You never loved me.
For it is in love
that we grieve
    So
     Deeply.

Do not honour my life,
Without shedding a tear.

If you *truly* knew me,
And want to honour me,
You will do so with raw,
                          Wild

                                    Unbound

                                              Tears.

The kind of tears
That pull you onto your knees.

We will meet again
In the beautiful landscape
Of the *Soul*.
You can find me there, but first, you must grieve.

GRIEF & GRACE

Grief is a form of generosity, which praises life and the people and situations which we have lost. Grief that praises life shows the depth of our appreciation for having been given life enough to begin with, to experience both love and loss and that with all the mistreatment we humans give to the earth, **we still have this amazing unlikely opportunity to actually speak and bathe in the Divine.**" *– Martin Prechtel*

I've spent the majority of my life intimately dancing with grief; with all of its faces. I was born into grief, because I was born into death. Very shortly after I arrived earthbound, my primary environment was haunted by the Monster. Let's call this monster, cancer. The monster consumed, tortured, and dehumanized my birth father. He was the ripe old age of 26 and at the peak of his hockey career when he was emasculated by the Monster.

It took him down fast and hard. Leaving him blind, devastated, and anguished with tumours protruding from his head. He looked scary. My father did not die peacefully, and my mother, did not grieve. I absorbed it all. Confusion, pain, terror, anguish, and death. Too young to cognitively understand what had just happened, I was shown how to ignore, pretend, and silence the wails of grief.

Until many years later, grief came knocking at my soul's door. The tides were strong, and they pulled me along the current. This intimate relationship with grief lasted for 10 years – albeit it started when I was born. When the current pulled me under, I did not anticipate the journey that lay ahead.

My primary pain, imprinted at birth, was asking to be known and integrated. One does not experience grief through the rational mind, one is experienced *by* grief. I could not think my way through, I had to *feel* my way through until the core wound was felt. Feeling was not my normal currency, as is for so many of us. To feel in this profound way destabilized and frightened me – Would I go insane? Lose absolute control? What if it never stops? Thoughts swarming around like buzzing bees entering their hive. I was not shown the territory of grief, nor how to navigate it. I had to learn from grief – *She taught me.*

Sure, we can talk about grief academically, and I have spent years consuming written material on grief, desperate to understand what it was that I was experiencing. Yet, to truly know the beauty, power, and transformative potency of grief, we must get out of the rational and enter the heart. I offer you this gift. It may not speak to your grief, but it speaks to my grief. And how else do we understand something that is in essence, other worldly and destructive in force, unless we share our stories of these lived experiences.

We begin at the end, when I was 42 years old, and we spiral throughout time.

If wounds could be tended to in this way, with the space to be present to what is arising; and deep grief encouraged and seen as a birthing process; then perhaps humans might, just might, experience an internal state of peace and quietude. Like a new blank canvas to which they can paint an inspired

life picture, gathering the wisdom from their pain
and using it to align with goodness, with a life
motivated by love. This is my deepest hope.

Grief blows open the heart. Period.
There is nothing more to understand.
It just *is* the medicine for the Soul to be known,
to itself.

The emotion of grief is both devastating and
rewarding. Having kept it at bay for 33 years, I was
not taught how to grieve, yet I should have been
surrounded by it. Growing up it always felt as if
there was something 'off' and yet, I could never
put my soul-print on it.

Physical and psychological pain was something I
experienced often, but I prided myself in knowing
that I could 'handle' it. Handling it meant not
crying. I was a tough girl, a tomboy, an adventurous
child, a strong girl, an athlete, afraid of nothing
really. Yet, my emotional heart was always
vulnerable and sensitive; I learned to protect it by
letting little in.

If love remained at a distance, then I would never
hurt - so I believed. I did love, to the best of my
ability. Noting that loving is different from being
loved, or more so, being love. It was the energy
of grief that opened my heart and taught me this
difference.

If I loved, I was in control. To allow others to love me, felt more vulnerable; and being love, felt the most vulnerable of all. I learned this difference after my third child was born. You see, to love another with your entire being and receive the love of your child, brings an experience of much joy.

Yet in that joy, I also felt the vulnerability and fear; a knowing that death is inevitable. I believed that if I closed my heart, I would not feel the pain of death. This is an illusion. For to remain closed is more painful than to love and be loved; risking and knowing that one day there will be a loss, yet the joy of love is worth the risk.

The experience of grief was amazing (I can say this now) although absolutely unbearable, it provided an opening into my interior world. Grief, I believe, is the motivating emotion that keeps the momentum of growth moving forward; it is the contraction for your labor.

While in grief, it is almost impossible to believe that you are being propelling forward, for it feels like glue. The heavy weight of grief slows you down and for some, drowns. This is a necessary part of the birthing process - you must slow down. The pace of normal rational life is too fast for such an endeavor. Labor takes you outside of 'normal' and catapults you into unfamiliar terrain, as does grief.

To grieve is to heal, shares Miriam Greenspan, in her honest and real book *Healing Through the Dark Emotions*. Although this statement speaks truth, those who have braved the depths of despair and grief may have lost vision of this notion. For in the chaos, filled with an overwhelming amount of energy and pain, we may sometimes forget that this is the experience of metamorphosis.

There is purpose in the pain.

I was struck by the waves and intensity of grief a few years back. I grieved the death of a life that I once knew; I grieved for my children and I grieved for my home. I was beginning the descent, for that which I once identified with, that which created a sense of safety and purpose in my life, was now gone.

The physical relocation was the first catalyst that brought me into contact with grief. This opened the floodgates as my heart and soul began to bleed, and from this place I spiraled into my very own dark night of the soul. At times, I wondered if the reason we have rivers is due to all the weeping souls. If all the tears were captured, I wondered how vast the waters would flow.

We all carry a pain-story and the grief of which I speak of arises from these stories. Although so personal to you, it is these very experiences that have brought you/me to our knees. Let me elaborate, when a life experience rattles your core, sometimes it is so overwhelming that you find yourself collapsing in humility to that which is beyond your comprehension. I call this the Mystery.

I am speaking of the kind of life experience that puts you face to face with an internal pain so great that words could never do it justice – and it doesn't matter what the details are. It just is, because it broke you. Even in defining these kinds of life experiences, you lose something, something very sacred to your internal world. Words reduce and diminish the intensity of it all, and yet many find themselves searching for someone to listen to their story – without judgment, or a need to change anything (perhaps this is why I became a psychotherapist).

These pathways are pivotal to the growth and transformation process of our human heart and soul. Death, a natural cycle, provides us with an experience that reminds us of our impermanence. It is not always a physical death that causes us to grieve. Other metaphorical deaths such as: the death of an identity, a belief system, a community, a relationship, or a life once known are equally valid. And deeper yet, with horror to even write it, are the soul deaths caused by the fracturing of one's being through detonating deeds – evil acts.

Each of these experiences speaks to you

differently, and when you allow the pain of the
loss to move through you, you connect with the
precious experience of grief. In the pain lives a
gem; and when surrendered to, will transform you.

I call this gem, *grace*.

Many are so afraid of the pain of grief and despair;
simply look at our cultural norms. We deal
with pain by numbing, drugging, avoiding, and
suppressing. Yet, it is the resistance to the pain,
which cultivates more pain, as already expressed.
Grief ignored, feeds the darker emotions
(depression, shame, anger, fear, and guilt). There
is a way to navigate the unknown and untamed
terrain that grief has on the heart and soul.

My soul journey involved tremendous loss in a
rather short period of time. The loss of my home
roots and community was just the beginning. Each
experience of loss, layered on top of the other,
cultivated an energetic weight so heavy that
eventually I collapsed. It became too much to bear.
On the surface, the collective losses I experienced
do not appear to be destabilizing. In fact, much of
what I lived through are shared experiences and
'normal' for many. As for so many of us, I too was
caught up in the belief that what I am experiencing
does not deserve the emotional attention; it is not
as bad as what 'others' live with. I struggled to not
believe that I was selfish for collapsing in my grief.

And, in the end, a part of me perceived my great collapse as a sign of weakness.

Why is it that we tend to not only compare our wounds, but diminish the degree of soul pain we experience? When this mindset persists, cognitive dissonance gains traction and we lose the opportunity to connect and heal.

Who knew that uprooting my family and leaving my community and homeland would cause the dam to break? Years of tears exploded out of my heart, confused and rattled by it all. I started to drink to numb the pain, all the while, trying to find my new footing on unknown territory as a mother of three. Nothing familiar, nothing normal, alone on pioneer land I continued to try, with all my force, to swallow my tears. Choking on my pain, nothing I had once done to ease my pain was working.

All of which resulted in the death of my 13-year marriage and the immense financial stress to find my way as a stay-at-home, now single, mother. Having raised our family on a low income for years, I didn't have a clue as to how I would pay for housing, let alone all the family needs. At this stage of the game, although I was collapsing even more, I was still holding my head above water, still under the impression that I could 'get through' and stay 'strong'.

The next blow to my ego came crashing down
with the loss of my identity as a Traditional Birth
Attendant (TBA). Having spent the previous ten
years studying and immersing myself within the
field of birth and spiritual midwifery, my entire
identity was tethered to this concept of self. I
believed that the one thing I had going for me
was this path, and even if all else was crumbling
around me, I could anchor in the knowing that I
had purpose.

That buckled, during which time I faced my
greatest fear as a birth attendant - I bore witness
to a mother's greatest devastation. Her unborn
never breathed earthbound. Not only did I have
a psychotic break after this event, I experienced
prosecution and shunning. Resulting in a terror
to venture out into public; waiting for the witch
burning. I felt this deep in my bones. This identity
did not want to die; she clung on with all hope.

As my sense of self depleted in strength, and my
mind convinced me that I was fundamentally bad,
I found myself choosing oppressive relationships,
resulting in more trauma. At the lowest moment, I
wandered the streets at night, questioning where
I would sleep and with whom? At this stage, the
mother I once knew, was no longer present within
me. She too had died.

In this pit of chaos, I was acquainted with the
underworld. I unleashed my sexual energy in ways

that defeated me, I poured toxicity into my body in a manner that was so foreign, and each day, I barely recognized the woman in the mirror.

I hung up my honor and walked soulless into the darkness. Where does one go when they can no longer tolerate the pain anymore? One must go deeper, allowing the self to be shattered.

This is exactly what I did, as I could no longer fight the collapsed heart. Having never navigated these emotions before, the traumatic grief flooded my being like a tidal wave that engulfed me. Bare and stripped naked, challenged to face all that I knew and once identified with, I ventured into this unmarked territory with one key element – *a belief that there is purpose in the pain and that I would find myself.*

There had to be some Truths I could hang onto while life as I knew it was crumbling under my feet. The Truth I kept coming back to are the principles of Quantum Midwifery, taught by one of my great teachers. I could *still* trust in birth. And, if I could trust in birth, I could trust in Life.

And, so I looked around for metaphors to guide my way through the despair.

My life had become very unfamiliar as my heart continued to peel back its armour. Even though I was left drowning in my tears, praying for someone to save me, I knew all I could do *was ride the waves* of the grieving contractions and go head on into the pain. In the same ways I became one with the pain during the labour of my third child. In which I saw, with my inner eye, that all we are made up of is space. My pelvis turned into particles colliding in a vast empty body of spaciousness. I knew without a doubt in that moment that what I saw, was Truth.

I took that knowing and applied it to my anguishing soul. I was convinced I was going to give birth to my Soul (whatever that meant). There was no escaping, no drug that would stop the flow, there was only experiencing with an enormous amount of *presence*.

Alone in my grief, as I let the waves crash into me, I was finding my way. At this stage I was still dealing with the challenges in my life; I had not yet touched my historical pain. It is true that we peel back the layers like an onion, slowly getting to the core wound.

In this, I navigated the labor pains of my life. As hopelessness surrounded me, I remembered the wisdom that my labors and each birthing mother had taught me. I recalled the teachings of my path and I learned how to midwife my grief, albeit that I questioned all my teachings with scrutiny.

In the end, I became the midwife for my Soul's birth.

A voice within, the voice of the Midwife spoke to me and whispered to my soul:

"Surrender dear One, and float above the pain"
"Ride the waves and let them overwhelm you"
"You are never alone; many have gone before"
"There is a way through, let the grief contractions take you away"
"Stop thinking, experience in total, let go"
"I know it is painful, there is purpose in the pain"
"Transformation happens from an altered state of consciousness"
"Allow yourself to become undone, you will be okay"
"Trust the process my Love"
"Fighting the sensations creates more pain"

In the darkness of my despair and gut-wrenching pain of my heart's cry, I learned to surrender in ways unimaginable. Angels carried me away (I like to believe this to be true). Moreover, I trusted in that which was beyond my mental and ego grasp. I deeply wanted to be cradled and rocked, held with loving presence. I had to learn how to hold myself; to love myself anew.

The power and courage that stems from slaying the demon of grief is miraculous indeed, and forever with you. Grief is a gift for transformation when received in *her* fullness. To be the Witness and the Midwife of your own soul's journey is to know the magical power of the force that lies within us all.

This inner *knowing*, a wisdom innate to all, illuminated the way.

The challenge many of us face is a disconnection that has severed the tie to this inner *knowing*. We have lost contact with our interior world; the wisdom within has been silenced. This shows up as doubt, insecurity, fear, anxiety, confusion and disembodiment. When we are stuck in these limiting feelings, we engage in the holding pattern.

Listening to the voice within is one thing. Acting in accordance to its message is another. I think many of us can listen, and we do hear. We choose to not act because to do so would result in going against our 'normal' environment. We, especially as women, have been conditioned to ignore the wisdom within and never question the world out there. We have been silenced.

Grief heals those severed vocal cords.

Journal Entry

You've been waiting your entire life for this moment. A moment of authentic expression of love and grief. A moment of acknowledgement. A moment of shared experience. A moment of humanity. Separated from this expression since birth. I've been waiting, waiting, as if there has been a wall of plexiglass standing between myself and my felt experience. A veil. A shield. A barrier. Protecting me from my grief, and the unprocessed grief of those around me.

I never grieved. She never grieved. *They* never grieved. Waiting for the moment in soul-time when the flood gates would open, and my Being was strong enough to be with the soul pain. This time was now. I let my mom be with her experience. I let myself be with her experience. And, we shared in experience. What do I do now?

How do I let

       This

           Be?

How do I let

       This

           Change

               Me?

What is there to be changed? I'm afraid to breathe.
I'm afraid to miss 'it'.

I'm afraid to let

                it

                    go.

I've been waiting. Waiting for what? Waiting to be
held. Waiting to be seen. Waiting to be heard. My
soul has been waiting. The last stone turned over.
The core wound expressed. The wounded soul,
soul that has been giving rise to my entire life path.
Every angle, every decision, every experience,
every behaviour. Everything driven by this unfelt
place – that deeply wanted to be seen. What is *this*
that wants to be seen? Is it seen, or is it felt?

She has been felt.
There *is* clarity.
There are no narratives.
It just is.
It just was.
It is okay.

I'm okay.
I'm okay.
I'm okay.
I'm okay.

It is *all* okay.

The depth of soul pain that I have felt has been immense. Not unusual, but immense.

For me, does it qualify? Is it 'enough' pain? But what about others who have endured worse? natters my mind. I felt. I dealt. Now what? Maybe there is a pause – a quiescence.

Is this the birth?
The new life?
The shedding of the skin?
Is this *it*?

I know that there will be more shedding; this is the nature of life. But maybe for a while I can settle into my soul. Relish in this work well done. Be with my 'self', all of myself, for the remainder of my life. No longer running away from this pain; from this yearning. No longer needing to fill it or fill anything.

I'm okay.
I'm okay.

What will it feel like to no longer be running?

Sure, I notice I still experience fear. We all do. Our bodies are programmed to feel our fear. To seek security. To escape danger. That is what our biology does.

What we perceive as danger is dependent upon our past, coupled with our historical experiences. All stemming from those 4 fears; to escape and avoid feeling those four fears.

Fear of annihilation.
Fear of abandonment.
Fear of going crazy; mad.
Fear of being evil; bad.

All of which lead to a death.
If I am annihilated, I'll die.
If I'm abandoned, I could die.
If I go crazy, I die from myself.
If I'm evil, my soul has died.

No one will love me, and I will die.

Our biology wants to live. Or does our consciousness want to live? Death is perceived as extinction. Extinction of living. But our soul cannot be extinguished. Or can it?

Consciousness is eternal. We are afraid to die to our attachment of our concept of ourselves. We are afraid to die to our perception of reality.

Fear is triggered by all of our tightly formulated thoughts about the nature of what we are experiencing. It feels so real. It lives in our cells...

This

     Fear

         Of

             Death.

I have lived frozen in terror of death. In my bones, death meant finality. End of connection. End of relationship. End of bond. End of person. Are we afraid of death? Or are we afraid of the pain associated with the end of these love bonds? We are not given hope that there is an eternal connection that the relationship can continue. We may 'believe' in a concept about 'life after death', but most often we do not *know* how to maintain a bond after death. We grieve the relational, and maybe grief opens the doorway for a spiritual bond. Does this bond come through love? Maybe. It feels nice to think this. But really, it is rare to achieve. So, how do we exist knowing that there is a fragility to human life? What is our purpose as a species?

To feel deeply.

Consciousness wants to feel. It wants to experience, and express and be expressed. It wants to love and be loved. What does *it* know – consciousness? It knows more than all my thoughts.

Thoughts are merely constructs; we made them up. We make them up. So, what are these words, if not thoughts strung together. How can we decipher between thoughts as perceptions and original thought?

Is consciousness no-thought?
Is consciousness experiential.
          Awareness.
                    Movement.

But words denote a thought. Words give rise to a perception. Do words give meaning? Create meaning? Are words the scaffolding of the architecture we call life? Without words, without thought, there is no-thing. What am I supposed to do now?

You'll know. As it unfolds, you will know.
Says the *voice*.

One step in front of the other. One moment at a time. You'll know. You watch what arises.
You listen. You act. That *is* it.

Each moment is a moment; in noticing, observing, listening, acting. Humans take action; action is Soul animated. We don't act, because we are afraid. We listen, but we do not hear, because we are afraid of knowing. We lose ourselves in the narratives. These narratives, the Maya, the great *illusion*.

FROM VICTIM TO *Victorious*

"We grow primarily through our challenges, especially those life-changing moments when we begin to recognize aspects of our nature that make us different from the family and culture in which we have been raised."
~ Caroline Myss

I was first introduced to the concept of *Woundology* while reading Caroline Myss's writings, but I dived into it more intimately during midwifery studies with Whapio from The Matrona. I was captivated. The word implies the study of 'wounds', more so, the fascination we humans tend to have with our pain stories. To be clear, I am not talking about physical wounds, rather, our psychic wounds. The notion is that humans tend to fester in their wounds, often resulting in illness.

Why do we do this – fester in our pain stories? A question I have contemplated for a long while.

Clearly, we are either 'getting something' out of our pain story or we are in need of something that we have yet to receive. Let's consider the fact that when we have a physical wound the body usually takes care of it on its own. True, our attention is drawn to the area that is infected or injured. However, there is a trust that the body will regenerate and restore itself back to health.

Now, the game changes if we are dealing with a physical illness. There is a gap in our minds and beliefs that occurs between physical injuries – like a cut or gash – and physical illness. With physical injury most humans *believe* that the body will take care of it. However, with illness our *beliefs* vary. Some believe that the body heals from illness, others believe that without external help, the body won't restore itself. Others, like myself, fear that death is around the corner.

Remember that I was born into cancer that devastated and destroyed my family's sense of health and security. I was imprinted with a belief that illness results in death. Our *beliefs* inform our perceptions. If we *believe* that our body can heal from illness, we are more likely to heal from that illness. If, however, we *believe* that illness results in death, we are more likely to be trapped in fear and anxiety. As such, we become trapped in our angst. Rising our stress levels to toxic extremes and in turn, 'feeding' the illness.

Taking this one step further, when it comes to mental and emotional health, that gap is even wider. Something about our psychic health feels impossible to imagine that we can change or heal. The body appears obvious, because we can see it. However, the illusiveness of the mind or the psyche can feel foreign or untouchable.

We touch it through our stories – the inner realm of the psyche. Voila, here we are now, trapped in the telling and re-telling of our painful stories.

Trauma theory informs us that telling our story does not resolve the trapped trauma that is frozen in the system. The re-telling of our pain stories produces stress chemicals and those stress chemicals are very familiar; they remind us that we are alive. Endorphins are the addictive by-product that materializes after experiencing a trauma; this is why it is said that we become addicted to being in a state of high stress.

It is disturbing to think that we get a rush of euphoria after a traumatic event. However, this is the body's way of detaching us from too much pain and preparing us for death. It is known as feigning death, to prevent death. Although this book is not about the science behind trauma theory (although I have written tons on that topic), I do want you to understand that we can become addicted to our chaos and living in our stressful holding patterns. Resulting in the need to fester in our pain stories. Here in lies, the concept of Woundology.

There is a dangerous fine line we walk as healers. We seek to uphold the victim to rise victoriously. To step outside of their wounded skin and claim their wisdom. There is a difference between identifying with your pain story vs sharing it in wisdom. I share this because your story does matter. But what matters even more is *how* you are sharing it.

Why are you sharing it?
How are you sharing it?
What do you leave out and why?
What do you add and why?
What are seeking to 'get' out of sharing it?
What do you need from the other after sharing it?

What parts still activate you while sharing it?
What parts are still in your inner dungeon?
Do you use your story to attach to others?
Do you share your story to teach?
Do you share your story as just that, a story?
Are you still seeking to punish?
Are you still seeking to wound?
Are you still seeking to harm?
Are you still seeking something?
What is that something?

As you can see there are many reasons why we share our story (or don't). To become conscious of the agenda is the medicine. Healing our soul wounds takes a ton of patience and compassion. Woundology is not suggesting that you never share your story. It is asking you to take charge of your healing and realize that your soul wound is activated, and leading the way, until you become conscious of it.

Many perish along the way and never claim the burning skull, as depicted throughout the glorious story of *Vasilisa*. In which the Cinderella-like character claims her power is symbolically portrayed by the skull of fire leading the way. I believe that we all have a fire skull to claim that will light the way. The skull can symbolize much. I like to imagine that it represents the death of our wounded ego and that we have slayed our inner demons to claim that which is our birthright.

We cannot claim our inner power if we are stuck indulging our wounds.

To embody the elements of the victorious after having been scorched in the human fires, is no task for the faint of heart. To rise in wisdom, means that we have tended to our wounds but no longer feed the pain stories. To feed means to indulge in the attention we receive from our woundedness. Truthfully, I struggled with this for years. I actually experienced a ton of anger towards my Teacher because of this concept. I sat in heated circles as hot topics like abuse, oppression, racism were unpacked. Nothing comfortable about suggesting to someone that they are indulging in their cultural or familial wound. I remember one student walking out and never returning to the program.

I don't think the concept of 'feeding our wounds' is meant to be understood in the mind alone. We have to drop into the heart of the matter. We need to engage the soul, and we need to *feel* into what it really means. If we indulge in our pain story and use it as ammunition or even passion for that fact, we are not healing it. I am not saying that people should not be held accountable for horrible deeds; they should be. Period.

In my psychotherapy work, when we land on a core wound, my client starts to become aware of all the ways the wound has served them. This is usually not a comfortable point in therapy.

Often, a client will pop out of the soulful place and jump into the rational mind. Reasoning with me. However, with gentle compassionate willingness, we go back into it. Underneath it all, there is a knowing that we/they/I have founded our identity from our wounds. Without our wounded story and all the beliefs that have been born out of them, we could have been annihilated. Our sense of self at least. There is no familiar ground to walk on. At the core, I have to come to know that almost all humans have formulated their sense of self, personality, perceptual lens, and interaction with external environment from their wounds.

Usually, when you float back far enough, there is often *one* core wound. Every other wound is a repeat of the core wound. The next thing you know, you come face to face with realizing that your entire life was scaffolded in an attempt to distance 'yourself' from this core pain, as a result of the core wound. I vouch that the majority of humans don't like the idea of realizing that their life is actually a deck of cards that is about to fall. However, it is in this great fall that Truth shows up.

Although 'Woundology' is a sensitive topic to broach. We love our stories and the perception that our stories make us who we are. Who would we be without stories? This is the wonderful question that the famous Byron Katie is known to ask. I invite you to consider it.

Within the new age communities, the term 'victim' is tossed around like a hot potato that no one wants to grasp for too long. The notion of being 'victim' to anything is frowned upon; it denotes weakness and misery. A kind of suffering that many of us try to run from. Let's differentiate between the term's victim, wound, suffering and victorious. As we move through our painful circumstances, we will encounter all of these.

There is a difference between being victim to something and identifying with our wounds. A wound is what surfaces, that which is exposed when we are injured. Physically this is obvious, soulfully it is invisible. The wound is the result of the harm. A victim is that which has endured the harmful deed or event. The victim, at the moment of injury, was *powerless* to escape the situation.

Suffering is the anguish that occurs when we wrap our sense of self up in our wound stories, when we sometimes cannot separate the self from the wound. Suffering is the result of *believing that we are no more than our wound stories*. Suffering is experienced as physical, mental, emotional, and soulful distress.

I have not yet met a human who does not have a victim story, in which they were wounded by an event or person big or small. Being victim to an experience is different than having a victim mindset.

It is the mindset that keeps us prisoner to the despair. Feeding the wound is a mindset. Viktor Frankl wrote so eloquently about this exact notion in his book 'A Man's Search for Meaning,' during which he deduced that meaning trumps the human need for survival, that even in the most outrageous and hideous circumstances – for Viktor it was concentration camps – the human spirit can still soar and thrive with the freedom to create meaning.

The mind seeks to assign meaning to all that we encounter. The meaning we attach to our life story differentiates between a victim mindset and one of wisdom. The quest is to shift out of the pain of the soul wound, to that of rising up with wisdom to share. This takes every cell in your body to choose to *believe* that it is possible. And we must *feel* our way through this process.

We tout the concept of resilience and post traumatic growth as a commodity we are entitled to experience; the expected gold at the end of the quest. Albeit true, humans are incredibly resilient because we are earthbound. It is not a given however, that all will rise from the embers of destruction and pain. To claim, with embodied conviction, that which was never destroyed in the chaos requires an inner fire ignited so that no amount of human turmoil will distract.

What I have been sharing thus far is all about excavating our deepest soul wound, bringing it to the surface for cleaning and care, and then witnessing it heal. The soul birth process is essentially the process of birthing a new self all the while tending to your deep wounds.

It is the wounds of the heart and soul that become the catalyst to the descent into the underworld - the tunnel of despair. It is the excavation of this wound and the proper care of it that facilitates the healing and soul-birthing process. Without coming face to face with this core soul wound, one can remain stuck in 'purgatory' and be overwhelmed with pain – the holding pattern.

Having said this, one must be mindful to not 'feed' the wound. In feeding the wound with toxic energy, poor-me mentality, or victim mindsets, the wound can fester and infect; healing is hard to achieve from this state. Yet something feels so good about the experience of feeding the wound, rather than feeding the heart.

In contemplating this idea, I questioned what happens when someone chooses to no longer engage the wound in this manner. What goes on within their internal world, to which they are able to make a different choice and see that they are stuck? What is it that drives you towards healing and wholeness? What is it that keeps you from moving forward? Why are we so afraid to heal?

I recall another time when I was in circle with other women and we were listening to a talk about 'woundology' – how if we live in our wounds we constrict, deplete, and cycle in suffering. Wounds need to be tended and healed. However, there is a fine line between feeding them versus nurturing and healing them. Allow me to attempt to speak to this difference.

Globally we are in crisis. We live in a global wound and there is a tendency to focus on this wound. Such as: environmental crisis, poverty, war and violence, overconsumption & consumerism, oppression and racism, and everything that encompasses these challenges. Some of us are conscious of it, others blinded by it.

This global crisis has become so normal that we barely realize the impact that it is having on our growth and evolution - both individually and globally. We remain trapped in a helpless state and the wound is the distraction. The Buddhist would say this is Maya – the veil of illusion.

I am, however, far more comfortable speaking to the individual wound and going internal, versus taking on the global wound. For it is true that what is experienced internally is experienced externally. I work with the internal map of reality, so to speak. In saying this, I encourage you to explore the difference between living in your wounds versus noticing them, so to respond.

According to author Caroline Myss, Woundology is a global crisis and it is encouraging people to stay stuck in their wounds.[2] There is money to be made in feeding our wounds and it keeps the human race disempowered. Staying stuck in our wound story is also another example of our narcissistic culture – especially in North America.

The self-help industry has skyrocketed, and so has the use of Prozac. The global system that has power, does not want to see our human race healed, for this would be a power threat to this operating system. When in fact, it would lose this power immediately if we all started to deal with healing our interior soul wounds, real power would return, and the potential for global healing would increase.

When you meet new people what do you connect about? Usually, within the first 5 minutes or so, we connect about our wounded stories, whether it is lack of money, childhood trauma, abuse, relationship problems, men, women, and health/ diet. There is something comforting about meeting people who share a similar complaint; it tends to make us feel better. We often experience a sense

---

[2] Myss, C. (2017). *Anatomy of the Spirit: The Seven Stages of Power and Healing.* New York: Harmony Books.; Myss, C., Harvey, A. (2012). *Divine Rebels: Saints, Mystics, Holy Change Agents, and You.* Sounds True, Inc.

of relief just knowing someone else can relate. Clearly, we need to have our stories witnessed and heard to facilitate deep healing.

I noticed that this was true in my own life. When I no longer connected over my inner wounds, I started to connect with others over external global wounds. I asked myself: What would connection look like separate from our wounds? I went on an experiment, to consciously attempt not to be in the wounded stories – aside from my private practice. Personally however, I wanted to learn a new way to connect. And guess what, it was hard.

I didn't know how to connect without exploring something wound-related. I thought it made me deep, important, or that the conversation was meaningful. I had all the reasons why connecting over wounds was beneficial. When I learned how to quiet my mind, and direct my energy with attention, I discovered that connecting in this way is still. I was uncomfortable with this stillness and quiet between myself and the others. I wanted to fill the space. And that meant filling the space with wounds (even if it seemed productive). Eventually, I found a balance. By no means do I feel untangled from this human imprint – to relate over our wounds -I am however far more conscious of it.

So, what is your wound feeding?

It is imperative to ask yourself this question. What are you gaining by staying stuck in your wound story? You will be surprised to learn that you are gaining some form of attention, love, satisfaction, or comfort - just to name a few.

Therefore, when I speak about woundology, I am speaking about the desire to grow the wound, grow the story behind the wound and become comfortable framing your life around your wound(s). In this state, something in you believes that they matter. That you belong. I believe the reason why we relate in this way is because, fundamentally, our need for love, affection, attention and healthy energy are not being met. Culturally, we know no differently.

I propose, this mindset and practice of feeding our wounds rather than healing them is a distraction, a distraction from doing the work that needs to be done so that energy can be freed up. Once this energy is free, you are capable of functioning optimally as a human and this newfound quality could possibly start to support the necessary global shift many speak of. However, there is fear about this quality of change, for to operate from this kind of healthy power would change both our internal and external world as we know it.

As humans, we all have stories and some of these stories are very painful indeed; for this is part of growth and evolution, and they are important life experiences that should never be lessened, ignored, or devalued. We need to recognize that becoming comfortable with living in our pain bodies, as Eckart Tolle would say, is a real concern. We need to shift from comfort to discomfort to stir the internal need to let go and transform the wound, thus, resulting in the wound becoming the catalyst for growth rather than the reason for helplessness.

What happens if you leave a wound alone, having never tended to it?

In the beginning, you would experience the pain of it. It may be annoying and so you choose to numb it. However, if you never take care of it and address it properly, it infects, festers, and oozes puss. Sometimes, the wound is so bad that you need surgery, or a limb removed. The primary signal of pain is an indication that something is wrong and needs to be taken care of immediately.

Culturally, we tend to either ignore pain or medicate it, rather than excavating the self to discover what the pain is saying. When we do this, the pain brings our attention to the area that needs healing and mending. The soul need is no different; it carries the wounds of the system, the mind, the heart, the body, the core, the spirit etc. To ignore the wounds of the Soul can cause stagnation and infection.

So, I ask, what are you most afraid of? What do you need to do to acknowledge and tend to your life's labor pains? What has stood in the way? Where are you now? What are you feeling?

Letting go of our pain story is the first stage of going deeper within. It drops us into a different reality and takes courage to do so. What is your pain story? What feeds your pain body?

THERE ARE NO WORDS TO
DESCRIBE THE PROFOUND

How do you put words to something so profound,
without diminishing the experience?

There are no words.

That is all I kept hearing.
There are no words
When you touch the profound.

Just breath.
Take it all in
One breath at a time.

There are no words
to describe the profound.

My cells are pulsing and vibrating
My whole body is tingling,
Yet dense.

Alive.

I see my life in review
Flash forward

Flash backwards
Over and over again.

It all makes sense.

When I wake
Awaken
It feels like I am in a space suite
Bouncing and floating.

Ballottement.

Like a baby swishing
around in the amniotic sac
Sensing the atmosphere
About to be born.

I heard myself say to *Her*
I had to scrape it
Chip away the ice to find his grave.

And *She* said to me
Did you just hear what you said?

"You had to chip away at the ice to get to his grave"

The great thaw
That is what this is
No more frozen within
No more void haunting.

We do not understand the profound
We just *know* the profound
No words.

And as the *I*, am writing this
Bringing words to paper
The *I*, that is taking insight
Making sense out of it
The sense that this *I* has
when this *I* settles into her

Soul-home.

There are no words.
There are no words to describe the profound
There is only magic.

What is the significance of the grave?
I did not *know* this man called Father
He was not kept alive through story
But he was kept alive through Soul.

The great turning
The philosophers stone
Fairy tales,
She kept saying Fairy tales.

The living myth
This is what Fairy tales are
They tell the story

We are living
They tell a tale of magic
They tell the Soul's tale,
This *I* is telling
Her soul-story.

There simply are no words to describe the profound.

BIOLOGY, *Biography*, AND BIOSPHERE

"Your biography becomes your biology" – Caroline Myss

"We have a natural ability called neuroplasticity, which means that if we learn new knowledge and have new experiences, we can develop new networks and circuits of neurons, and literally **change our mind**." – Joe Dispenza

THOUGHT PARTICLES –
A METAPHOR

In the midst of a session with a client, there were dust particles floating in the air, catching the reflection of sunlight and thus filing the atmosphere with dancing particles of dust light.

Needless to say, this caught both of our attention. We were in the middle of a psychoeducational conversation about automatic thinking and how we become enmeshed with our thinking. Resulting in the deep belief that we 'are' what we think.

I was explaining the term decentering as explained throughout the Mindfulness Based Cognitive Behavioural Therapy (MBCT) theory. Decentering is a principle notion that suggests the act of moving away from our thoughts so that we can begin to notice them as separate from the 'self'.

It occurred to me to use the dancing dust particles as an example and metaphor.

In this moment we could see the dust particles for what they were – flecks of particles in the air moving around in response to air movement. We both agreed that they are always there; however, most often we do not notice them. We are in a constant relationship with the dust particles because they are a part of the environment. Sometimes we even have a reaction to them, like coughing or sneezing. And generally speaking, it rarely occurs to us that the sneeze is a result of breathing in the flecks of dust.

Now, let's imagine for a moment that these dust particles represent thoughts. Lots of them. Swarming around your head and constantly in your environment. They cannot be escaped, in the same way that you cannot get rid of the particles in the atmosphere.

What happens when you begin to notice that there are a TON of thought particles floating around the atmosphere of your mind? What might happen if you imagine taking all the thoughts that fill your mental landscape and placing them in the floating dust particle so that you can 'see' them from a different perspective?

For my client, she began to recognize that thoughts are just there – always.

Thus, each dust particle is a representation of a thought bubble. When the 'self' can take a step back from the thought (decentering) then you (the self) can begin to notice how invasive and prominent your thoughts can be. In so much that you can begin to notice that you are swarmed by them, at all times. In essence, just like dust particles, there is no getting rid of thoughts. They are constantly permeating our space.

My client went as far as suggesting that in her experience the thought particles had colonized her mindscape. They had taken over and taken charge. This notion of 'feeling colonized' by thought particles was a powerful insight. It suggested that there was an opening to the possibility that her thoughts/your thoughts are part of the atmosphere but that they have been allowed to take up far too much space. Like any dusty situation, we need to 'dust' the environment and cleanse it, clearing the space for fresh air. Sometimes dust settles and builds up and causes problems. This buildup is often an allergen and for some people, is a symbol of stagnation and not tending to the space.

In keeping up with the metaphor, our thoughts can pile up one on top of the other, potentially causing one to feel weighted down, anxious, or overloaded. Those thought particles are just hanging around in the mind sphere, not really moving out of the way, creating a dust bunny pile of debris. The debris is often filled with unprocessed emotions and gives rise to a state of being. i.e. mood.

What would happen if those ignored thought piles got stirred up, swept up, and redistributed into the larger atmosphere?

This is exactly what starts to happen when we move away from the thought pile, stop identifying the self as the dust pile of thoughts in the corner, and recognize that the thoughts are merely particles of 'dust' that truly have no meaning until we assign the particle with meaning.

They are just that – thoughts.

Beginning to pay attention to your relationship with your thoughts is a key ingredient in one's path towards healing and mental health. I know that this has been written about a million times over. For some of us, however, it can take a lifetime to absorb what is being read. Taking a concept and applying it to our lived experience is far different than absorbing content. Often, when we read, the material is taken in as merely more thoughts.

My experience in the moment of noticing the dust particles was an AHA moment for both myself and my client as a visceral and visual experience of *knowing* that thoughts were merely dancing particles that existed with or without the 'self'. They are just there in the atmosphere. If we have a brain, we experience thoughts. But we are not our thoughts, yet we tend to merge with our thoughts as an absolute truth of reality. Although the thought that we attune our attention *feels* true and real, there is a plethora of floating around thoughts to choose from at any given moment. What causes us to zoom in on a particular thought? What informs that choice?

Where we attune our attention, our energy
follows. Thus, as we zoom in on a particular
thought there is a consequence; it has an effect.
The act of being distracted by a thought, or a
string of thoughts, pulls us away from the moment.
The present moment is no-thought, no- thing.
Awareness is no-thought, no-thing. And yet,
merging with a thought distracts from the present
moment and gives rise to an emotional experience
or felt expression.

As my client and I were paying attention to the
dancing particles of dust in the air, we practiced
zooming in on one small particle of dust light and
zooming out to take in the entire space of dancing
particles. In either situation, there was an act of
choice. If we consider this notion as it pertains
to our thoughts, we can begin to understand the
notion of 'choice' and 'choosing our thinking'. What
we are choosing is where to direct our energy and
attention; Whether or not we zoom the lens in on
a particular thought or not.

Before we become aware of this option, we are
existing in a space of automatic zooming per se.
We are not paying attention to which thoughts our
lens zooms in on. We just let the lens zoom in and
out at will – this is our imprinted biological will.
One could say, from this vantage point, that we
are not aware of the dust particles. They are there,
we just don't see them. The same holds true about

thoughts. They are there, we just haven't fostered the skill to notice them.

Just like dust is always there, whether we see it or not, so are thoughts. The key is not to banish thoughts, but to begin to notice them, realizing there is nothing unique about your thoughts.

We can imagine that there is a global community of thought particles available at all times.

So, the term 'notice your thoughts' albeit simple and direct, is incredibly hard at first. But once you notice how you are in relationship to your thoughts – enmeshed or decentered – you can begin to pay attention to which thought your inner gaze zooms in on. If you don't like that thought, you can zoom out again and take space from the thought. Again, realizing that the thought itself has not vanished, but rather, that it is no longer receiving your gaze. The thought doesn't die or shrivel up, it continues to exist in the atmosphere of thought particles.

In fact, it doesn't even matter *why* you zoom in on one particular thought. Rather, what is more important is realizing that you *are* zooming in on a particular thought. And now, you want to zoom out again. Practicing alternating the lens and the zoom is part of the art of mindful awareness.

A helpful tip: Remind the self at any moment 'Am I zooming in on any particular thought right now?

If yes, what is it? How do I feel when I believe that thought? What would happen if I took my gaze away from that thought for a moment? If I am not my thoughts, then who am I?

Two powerful questions to adjust the zoom and bring consciousness to the forefront:

1. What am I hearing myself say about this particular stressful situation?

2. What am I hearing myself say *about myself*, as it pertains to this stressful situation?

WORDS

Words
Are all I have
To express
That which seeks
To be heard.

Words
Misinterpreted
Misunderstood
Misrepresented
Who am I without
Words?

Who would I be
Come.
Words heal, damage
I love you, I hate you
Spoken
Undone
Words.

They are just words.
'Sticks and stones'
Who is the artist,
Without words?

Expressed through
Movement
Painting
Form
Song.

What is *it* that speaks?
Who is it doing,
the expressing?

What would happen
If we erased words,
Removed
From the tapestry of Life.

Who would you be without words?

Spoken in all forms
Silenced are the voices
Choked in the throat
Terrified to speak.

The seer sees.
The knower knows.
The sage speaks
Words.

WE ARE MORE THAN OUR BIOLOGY

"Sometimes we need to step back and allow a new reality to settle and integrate within us before setting out to heal the world. In fact, I have observed some healers and seers who have not given themselves sufficient time for their own healing. Frequently, they felt pressured to be selfless and put the wounds of others above their own." ~ Kristin Madden

I have been deep in the vortex of contemplative practices lately, posing some big questions as I sift through all the information gathered over the years. As a psychotherapist (more appropriately a Midwife for the soul) a day does not go by in which I am not seriously pondering the purpose of therapy; the purpose of awakening; the purpose of healing; and all that overlaps.

Setting 'imposter syndrome' aside, I often ask myself: Am I 'feeding' a wound or am I tending to the wound, so it can heal? How can I/you tell the difference? What does it mean to indulge a pain story?

Throughout my studies in Quantum Midwifery, I was taught some very wise principles which are transferrable to the field of psychotherapy and healing. As I have distilled them over the years, they are as follows:

- We have an innate wisdom in our biology that knows how to give birth(heal).
- We birth (heal) from an altered state of consciousness.
- Birth (healing) is a transformative experience.
- Interrupting the flow of the altered state of grief slows down the process.
- The key skill is presence.
- Trusting the process is paramount.

- Flow with the grief, do not force.

- Listen, do not preach.

- We all find our way, as long as we get out of the way.

- Learn to manage your energy and then, use it wisely.

To return birth back to the family, is to return power back to where it belongs – within each and every individual. And this was the guiding principle throughout my sacred midwifery teachings. Nothing about my learning was common, albeit traditional in the ancient root of the word. I knew I was learning about the Mystery of life during these studies, as we used birth as the sacred lens to understand the nature of Life itself.

Needless to say, this quality of learning was not always tangible in the modern profession of Midwifery. Much of what I learned contradicted modern Midwifery, which challenged my ego. I wanted to be a professional Midwife, but the deeper I went into the vortex of Quantum Midwifery, the more I understood that my soul would not let me. These teaching needed to be embodied. They needed to be understood in a way that traversed normal reality. I knew that by choosing to engage in the Quantum Midwifery teachings, I was being initiated as a spiritual Midwife. I would eventually learn how to lean on these teachings throughout my own soul birthing process.

The overarching notation has always been about holding the sacred as sacred and getting the fuck out of the way.

Healing is a sacred experience akin to childbirth. Holding space for someone to unfold their painful experiences so that they can begin to digest the emotional debris and make sense out of their chaos, is a laborious process.

For the soul to be open to the possibility of transformation, you must *trust* in the process.

In other words, you must believe that there is a 'way' through. Secondly, it is helpful to anchor in a guide/midwife to help facilitate a safe space for the unfolding of one's inner terrain (however, many find their way alone). Third, the midwife must understand soul pain and how to navigate through those tough places. Fourth, the midwife of the soul holds an unwavering presence that trusts in the journey of healing and transformation.

She knows that there is an innate wisdom that can guide the way, and thus, the Midwife gets out of the way.

Granted, none of this was taught throughout traditional grad school. Today there is a growing conversation about trauma-informed care and mindfulness as a healing modality. We are getting 'smart' about healing. We have peer reviewed journals talking about some of these healing modalities that facilitate lasting changes in people. We know more than ever about the long term impacts on lifestyle, behaviour, and health of Adverse Childhood Experiences (ACE); about resilience; about how unresolved trauma is at the root of mental illness, addiction, and disease; about the intergenerational impact that racism, oppression, abuse and poverty has on subsequent generations; about epigenetics and gene expression; about nutrition and gut health; about exercise and brain health. We know so much; information is at our fingertips. And yet we are still stuck in the past.

Dr. Joe Dispenza writes about how our past informs our future[3] – informs how we think, feel, and behave. Further, how our biology is imprinted in utero. Our entire nervous system is being programmed, while we are developing in the womb, by our environment (both current and historical). This notion sent me down another rabbit hole to seek to understand my own historical imprints, and how most of what I am healing is collective pain within my family lineage. This idea got me outside of my ego or small self, in

[3] Dispenza, J. (2015). *Breaking the Habit of Being Yourself: How to Lose Your Mind and Create a New One.* California: Hay House.

that I understood that what I have experienced in this lifetime is not personal.

It is all part of a historical program. And my biology is/was imprinted by this program.

Consider the notion that our painful lived experiences are not personal, this is not always an easy pill to swallow. Indeed, a paradox: on one hand the experiences are *personal* because they happened to you, and on the other hand, they are also impersonal because they belong to a historical lineage of embedded beliefs, feelings, and behaviours.

For example, the shame I can experience in my body feels unique and individual, yet it is in fact a shared experience throughout my maternal lineage. In fact, some of that shame is collective beyond my family and shared with other women. Or let's consider the belief that 'I am inadequate'. This too is a shared belief, yet I often believe it with 100% of my cells. It *feels* so real and true.

This leads me to pose the question: Where do I begin and end? What is mine and what is shared? My painful emotions feel uniquely mine. However, I intellectually know that they are a collective experience. So why am I/we so attached to the pain, the stories, the history? Why is it so hard to move beyond the painful past? What am I, are we, resisting? Why is it so bloody hard to remind ourselves that these grueling inner conversations and self-perceptions are goddamn lies?

Lies.

That is what they are. They are collective lies that are embedded into our psyche. And I have not met a human yet who has not struggled to dismember and untangle the web of interior lies. I question if there is a purpose in believing these sick lies – I am bad, wrong, dumb, stupid, inadequate, incapable, insufficient, unlovable, disgusting, helpless, hopeless. Is it possible that the purpose is to keep us distracted and small?

Consider this for a moment. When we are preoccupied with believing these fucking lies (Yes, I need to swear here to prove a point because I am pissed off at the destruction these lies have had and have on our psyches) Okay, I have digressed. Back to being distracted. The lies are all consuming, wreak havoc on our emotional wellbeing, cause us to be self-absorbed, too focused on the little self, incapable of being present with reality as it is. In other words, they fuck with the entire system – when we believe them with all our being, that is. And the result? Depleted, unattached, shut down, numbed out, anxious, an insecure human who struggles to keep her head above water. It literally drains us of life force. And I believe that this is potentially intentional. But if I start to unpack this, you might really think I am clinically delusional.

Yet, these lies are the delusion.

As I spiraled down this vortex, I found myself posing the following questions:

- Why do we believe these lies?
- Why is it so hard to stop believing them?
- Who would I be without the lies?
- What would I believe instead?
- If these are lies, what are the truths?
- How do I know that they are lies?
- What does it mean to heal?
- What if our greatest pain is, in fact the catalyst for awakening?

Joe Dispenza writes that we are addicted to the emotions of our past.[4] These lies I speak about produce an emotional response. It is further noted that until we move beyond the emotions of our past, we will forever be living from the past. Hence why we tend to find ourselves stuck in 'holding patterns' that resemble the last dramatic situation we were just in; the circumstances are different

---

[4] Dispenza, J. (2019). *Becoming Supernatural: How Common People Are Doing the Uncommon*. California: Hay House.

but the felt experience is same. From this point of view, we are living from our biological imprints.

How do we move beyond the biology?

This concept – living from our past imprints – fascinates me. My biological Father's death triggered a soulful journey of seeking in attempt to understand death. A 2-year-old cannot understand death, but my soul knew something. Apparently, at that age, we are not differentiated from our primary caregivers. I have read that when a parent dies during this stage of development a part of that child dies with the parent. When I heard this, a huge light bulb went off, igniting my energy body.

A part of me had died with the death of my father. This part not only died; it *experienced* his death.

This may sound crazy, or farfetched. But I will say this, I *know* it to be true. My body and soul understood what that statement meant. It was a game changer. It unhooked my primary wound and the tsunami poured through my being. I was calling my Spirit back home. I was releasing myself from the energetic cord that was still attempting to attach to my dead father. I understood on a cosmic level that I had been walking between worlds for 40 years.

So much clicked together after this realization, as this was the missing puzzle piece I had been searching for. I understood why I had been courting the altered state since I was very young. It started with prayer, in hopes that I could connect with my dead father through a 'heavenly father'. This led to spontaneous out of body experiences during adolescence and teen years (which frightened me). By the age of eleven I was guiding my classroom through progressive relaxation meditations. I thought it was 'cool' that if you went deep enough into the process you could not lift your body off the ground; you were glued to the earth. In grade seven, I wrote an essay on out of body experiences for school and thought it was normal teenage curiosity. I had already read the bible by that age and was angry that as a girl, I could not become a priest, so I left the Catholic church and tried other religions during my teen years. I was told that I could have a direct relationship with God, without going through a Priest, through Jesus – sign me up. Anything that would get me one step closer to understanding why this Jesus-dude needed my 'Daddy' in Heaven.

During my first year of college I took world religion and was blown away by all the similarities between the religions and therefore could not understand why we were still at war over whose religion was best. During this time, I studied kinesiology and performance psychology, and was fascinated by imagery (mind-movies) as a tool for peak performance. I was already actively practicing 'creative visualization' for peak performance in athletics, which resulted in a university scholarship.

I remember being taught in the 90's that the mind cannot differentiate between what is 'out there' vs what is 'in here' (i.e., inner reality vs outer reality). Thus, if you can see it and believe it, you can achieve it. My quest never stopped, and I continued to explore Shamanic traditions and Goddess Spirituality as healing paths. All along I would Vision, not knowing that I was Visioning. It all felt normal and familiar. Yet, after all this spiritual courting, I still found myself empty hearted. No contact with some Divine Intelligence that *took* my Father – or so I was told.

By this point I was all but 22 years old. Needless to say, I have been driven to connect to that which is beyond the biology – behind the veil, that 'thing' or 'space' I now call consciousness or the Field of All That Is.

Traditional therapy does not talk much about consciousness. It talks about symptoms, presenting problems, theory, modalities, treatment plans, case notes, and empirical evidence. Boring. Nowadays we can use the phrase 'mindfulness' to speak about attuning one's attention to what is happening internally and externally, moment-to-moment, without judgment. And here too, we are not talking about expanding consciousness – moving our attention outside of the cellular membrane of our biology and this atmosphere.

If two very important words – heal and consciousness – are left out of mainstream psychotherapy rhetoric, how confident can we be in the healing capacity of therapy and the schools that teach it? Did you know that many therapists have not gone to therapy themselves and rarely are they in any form of regular therapy? Some may have attended therapy because they had to for school, but once their hours were up, they stopped going. What does this say about the field?

How can we place our trust in a therapist who has *not* done their inner work of deep healing? Or a therapist who does not have a regular practice of expanding their consciousness? What about the notion that you can only go as far as your therapist has gone – they can only take you so far, depending on where they have gone within their internal terrain. We spend a lot of money on therapy or programs to 'get better'. I know I did. Close to the tune of 25K over the years. Did it help? Absolutely.

Trauma-informed therapy helped me get my brain back online. When I finally sought out professional help, I was literally losing my mind. I was concerned that I had early onset Alzheimer. My thinking was all jumbled up, it was difficult to formulate coherent thoughts. What came out of my mouth was not what my mind was thinking, it sounded disjointed. I had raging emotional outburst at my children for matters that were inconsequential. I could not tolerate light or sound. Any loud noise would send me into panic and trigger my rage button. I had to sleep with the lights on and needed background noise to soothe me to sleep. Driving was for the first time ever, challenging, as cars would zoom by and trigger tunnel vision. I could not handle the amount of external stimulation that was coming into my field of awareness, it felt like stress was pouring into me non-stop. I was flooded with cortisol and adrenaline.

Needless to say, I felt like I had no control in both my internal and external realities. I was a mess. Finally I succumbed to outside help. At first I saw this as defeat. Later, however, I recognized how important this stage of healing was.

I grilled my potential Psychologist over the phone before I committed to an in-person session. I needed to know that she could 'handle' me and my circumstances. I was paranoid too; did I mention that? She could meet me where I was at, and answered my questions to my approval, and so I committed to grueling psychotherapy and EMDR.

Initially I went about three times a week. Eventually that spaced out to weekly, and finally, monthly. In all, I think it took about 6 months to get my brain back, so to speak. And about two years to feel healthy and vibrant again. At which point I went back to Grad School to complete my studies in counselling psychology. Maybe this was a bit premature, as it used up almost all of my energy reserves. By when I had finished my practicum and had moved into a full-time private practice, I hit a wall. My system crashed, and hard. Compassion fatigue took over my biology and collapsed my system, reminding me that I need to take care of my energy.

I was working with trauma, full-time. I remember one advisor saying to me that perhaps I needed to walk away from the field of Trauma and focus on something lighter. I thought to myself, "Are you crazy?" This is what I have prepared myself for. I am *meant* to work with Trauma (Oh how our little self can attach to such grand ideas to be validated and important). Eventually, my body said no. And, this time, I knew that I had to listen.

What followed was a final push and unveiling of lingering core-wound stuff. I thought I had cleared it all, but as our Soul would have it, nothing is ever *done*. I settled into my interior world to be with the little one inside who was still holding onto the pain of death.

There she was. Alone in the darkness. And, I understood at this point, what it meant to be the 'carrier of the soul' within your family of origin. I was carrying the pain of my family – all of it. All of the unprocessed pain, grief, anger, death. I was holding it in hope of digesting it, so I could connect with my living family. If I could take away the pain, everyone would be okay, and I would feel secure and alive.

My greatest gift became my greatest adversary.

The thing that I have always been doing – perhaps born doing – was consuming me and killing me. Sucking my life force. I could no longer hold the pain of my family, nor could I hold the pain of my clients. This was a huge AHA moment.

I knew that I was not holding the painful stories of my clients in my mind. I did not anguish over some of the horrifying details, and I had a ton of capacity to be present with what was being presented in sessions. However, my Soul was doing all the work and it never rested. In fact, my two-year-old was doing the work. And, obviously, it is not the job of a two-year-old to hold the pain of people and our planet!

Thank the God/dess for this wake-up call. I know that if I had continued to do this invisible work, which was so *easy* and *natural* for me to do, I would have gotten very sick – like Cancer sick.

Although I had been *gifted* with an incredible ability to read the Field and *know* what was going on behind the personalities and masks that were at the forefront of nearly every human interaction, I was not equipped to handle the downpour of energetic information; especially as a wee child. I had no invisible helper (not to my knowledge anyway) who could show me the ropes of this mysterious terrain.

All I could do was feel, intuit, and interpret through my young lens. What I experienced was beyond words, because I had no words to describe the tension that was often present – the tension between that which was being presented and that which was *really* going on behind the eyes. This skill, if you can call it that, lends well to the therapist chair. I found a place to speak to what is being presented, and that which lives behind the human illusion. Sometimes this would be well received, other times, it would frighten. No one likes to know that they are being 'read' so to speak.

I didn't realize that this is what I was doing until my children started to tell me that their friends were intimidated by me because they could tell that I could just 'read them'. Of course, I wasn't always

consciously doing this. Remember that this *gift*
is the water I swim in. As I continued to clear out
the emotional debris from my past, my sensitivity
to this skill skyrocketed. I could no longer use the
numbing agents and defenses that would protect
me from the energetics of this world and the
people in it. I was porous now, and information
was pouring in at a lightening speed. Did this cause
my collapse?

Sifting through this material was daunting,
because it was not without the felt experience,
which for the most part, was/is filled with pain.
I was collapsing in the Kuan Yin compassion for
our planet, or maybe, more like Kali-Ma. My heart
was expanding as my interior made room for more
Love. However, the pain of our planetary suffering
imploded in on me. 'This is not mine' was on repeat
as I sometimes literally vomited devastation. I
would read about people who are transducers
for pain. They absorb the pain of others, digest it,
and churn it out of their system in an act of love
and compassion. Although I *felt* this to be true, my
mind could not accept it as a possibility. It seemed
like a cruel joke.

In an attempt to settle my wee one who had been
holding people's pain for far too long, I engaged
with her within my inner castle. I held her tightly
and let her know she does not have to do this
anymore, it is no longer her job, in fact it never

was her job. And I let her know that nothing she
does will bring her Daddy home to her. With that
she wept, I wept. I flooded the room with my tears
and my wails. The moaning and groaning that
accompanies death and grief was present, real,
tangible, and as if it had just happened yesterday.
To this two-year-old it was still happening. She
had been holding back her breath; her life force.
I let the tidal wave consume me, all the while, I
held her tightly for dear life. I knew my Soul could
handle this, and that it was time for her to sound
her hearts cry. I let her know that she will not die
in this pain, that she *does* not die, that it is safe now
to feel, and that she can rest now. And she did just
that, surrendered into my interior heart and curled
up to drink in the warmth of this interior love. She
could receive now. She could release now. She
could come home. Although therapy helped me get
my brain back, it was through these private tears
that I re-connected with my Soul.

What acted as my guide came from my
interior world – the life behind the mind's eye.
Accompanied by an unwavering *will* and *belief* that
healing is a birthright.

HEALING FROM AN ALTERED STATE OF CONSCIOUSNESS

If we give birth from an altered state of consciousness (more on this later) then it makes sense that we heal from an altered state of consciousness. Thus, as a therapist we/I must be incredibly comfortable navigating these altered states, both in a therapeutic space and within our own life. However, there is a profound difference between traditional psychology which focuses mostly on cognitions, treatment plans, modalities, and diagnostics, and soul healing.

Although the root word of psychology – psyche - pertains to the investigation of the soul territory. Modern practices seem to have lost this connection. Of course, if it cannot be measured or validated through double-blind research, the 'practice' or modality is disregarded. So much that has to do with the Soul is transpersonal and transcendental, thus, modern approaches to psychotherapy rarely touch the depth of the soul.

I am not saying that there is anything wrong with the mainstream evidence-based approaches to mental unrest. I am however suggesting that we call it something other than the 'study of the psyche' (psychology). I wish we were just straight forward about this and admit that the study of the Soul is far too complex and unapproachable. I mean seriously, the study of the Soul is a personal journey into one's own inner crevices; it is not something that can be taught in textbooks or understood through the rational mind alone.

And considering that few people are courageous enough to engage in a personal soul quest, it makes absolute sense that 'Soul' needed to be removed from the conversation throughout psychology studies. Further, if you can't teach something tangible, if it can't be measured to be understood, and if we cannot come up with a standardized treatment protocol, we can't make any money at it. So, the study of the Soul, or rather the institutionalization of these professional programs, would not make a ton of money from its students. Why? Because few would actually pass the course.

Soul work is hard fucking work.

And if you want to be a Midwife for the Soul (read: psychologist) but you are afraid of your interior dungeons and dragons, well you will become a shitty Midwife for the Soul. Fear breeds fear, and you can only take your client so far. And if each one of my clients engages an altered state of consciousness during our sessions together, and they are moving a large amount of soul pain and emotional debris, is it any wonder why I was exhausted by the end of the day? It is akin to attending 5 births back to back in one day, as a Midwife. This is unsustainable.

Which led me to pose another question: How do I/ we work sustainably so that I/we do not burn out as a midwife of the soul and please do not tell me to shield myself better?

What has occurred to me is that perhaps *we do not* need regular 1-1 therapy. In fact, a lot of the healing process can be done on your own time, at home. Although perhaps unconventional and puts me out of a job, I still think that there is truth in this statement. Yes, it would require a dedicated practice and process for healing. And perhaps a guide; I know the power of being witnessed and held. Being witnessed during these transformative times is powerful. Someone that can offer insight, encouragement, and suggestions that can help deepen the process – but is not responsible to do it for you.

When the soul is ready to integrate its core pain, it will emerge, and at this time I believe a few intense sessions can offer profound encouragement and love. Akin to attending a labour, the journey can be a few hours or a few days. Yes, a mama needs prenatal care to prepare for the intense journey that lies ahead. And this is exactly what my

Foundational Program is all about – preparing the soul and heart to come home to itself.

We want someone to hear our story – why?
We want someone to validate our feelings – why?
We want someone to take our pain away – why?
We want someone to give us something to make it stop – why?
We want someone to have the answers for us – why?

What do we want out of therapy?

I know I wanted to understand my suffering and I wanted to be validated. I didn't want to do it alone. I also knew I needed a modality that would help restore my nervous system, and it did. I felt better after a few sessions, but I was not done for years following. I needed to keep paying someone to help me figure out what I was experiencing and feeling.

I think that there is a more affordable way to do this. I think we can all share in this process of uncovering, restoring, and healing our painful pasts collectively.

Epigenetics. Have you heard the term?

It means outside, or on top of, the gene. The concept is that the environment informs genetic expression; not the gene itself. Each gene carries thousands of potential expressions generated by *perception* of environmental stimuli. We have both an internal and external environment and attached to each is perception. Our brain creates meaning. The meaning we attach to the environmental circumstances activates a genetic expression. This is a simplified 'Coles Notes' version of a complex topic of study. Dr. Bruce Lipton, in The Biology of Belief,[5] unpacks this in detail. The concept of epigenetics caused me to contemplate intergenerational trauma and family diseases.

The rabbit-hole I went down, looked and sounded like this:

If, how I perceive (make sense out of) my environment initiates the expression of my genes, then who and how was my lens of perception informed?

It is said that how you think and feel is informed by your primary environment, and further yet, how well you handle stress is informed in utero. Float back to your utero environment. Did you have a sense of what was happening for your birth mother at that time, how well she handled the stressors in her environment? Often when mothers hear this, they immediately absorb the message as mother-blaming. However, I floated

---

[5] Lipton, B. (2016). *The Biology of Belief: Unleashing the Power of Consciousness*, Matter, and Miracles. California: Hay House.

back even further within my interior landscape
and realized that the Mother is encapsulated by
layers of concentric circles of influence.

Think about this for a moment. The mother, while
incubating her baby, is in contact with her primary
environment. And who is in that space? What
is the dominant message? Is it driven by love or
survival? Moving further out from this immediate
space is another layer of influence.

This layer includes community, spiritual influence,
extended family. Each imposing their beliefs and
ways to make sense out of life circumstances.
This influences the Mother and thus, encodes the
growing fetus – You. Moving even further out,
environmental influence based on place of origin,
political views, financial circumstances, all of which
influence each subsequent layer. Finally, way out,
encircling it all, is the dominant worldview.

What is and was the dominant worldview while
you were incubating in your mother's womb?

From what I have gathered, the dominant
worldview is one of great fear – to consume
and conquer at all cost. This fear penetrates
each layer, resulting in an imprint that is born in
fear. This core fear hooks us into survival mode,
generating a ton of toxic stress material. Some of
us have additional layers of traumas accumulating
during childhood which send our system into

overdrive. In turn, resulting in a core imprint of high stress, fear, and disconnection from self and place, eventually resulting in a perception about self and environment that sounds like: I am bad; I am wrong; It is my fault; I am inadequate; I am helpless; I am incapable, to name a few. Without surfacing this deep imprint, the world as you know it, revolves around these beliefs.

It is said that our past predicts our future, until we become aware of it.

Think about this for a moment. If you were born into a field of chaos, trauma, uncertainty, neglect, lack, or oppression, you came into a field of pain. That environmental field of pain was all you knew – it was the water you swam in. Some people do not like it when I voice this part, but at this stage of development, you had no choice or control to change your environment. You were 100% dependent upon your primary environment and care givers to keep you alive.

As a child you are truly a victim to your circumstances. For many, this is too painful of a truth to broach. We like to imagine that we can bypass the pain of our past. However, until we become conscious of it, everything is born out of this primary wounding. When I say everything, I mean your way of thinking, feeling, and behaving in the world around you. Yes, this includes your personality.

But what about those who were born into a field of love. Love definitely buffers the impact of the imprint. For those of us who were born into an environment in which our primary attachment needs were met, our basic physical needs were met, we were seen, heard, and valued and were met with a calm and connected loving presence to attune to. Research suggests that, in these circumstances, we have strong building blocks for wellness and health. This means that those of us who were met with this quality of care have great capacity to tolerate high amounts of stress before becoming destabilized and dysregulated. Those of us who have absorbed a core imprint of love, most often hold core beliefs such as: I am loved; I am valued; I matter; I belong; I am allowed; I am important; I am safe, to name a few.

To cross the river of pain and embody the loving core beliefs from above, is the work I am talking about. This is *the* most challenging act because it requires that you change the frequency with which your entire cellular being is operating from. You cannot change your thinking alone. You must *know* in your body that you matter; you belong; you are loved; you are safe; you are valued. To *know* is to feel and experience. For those who came to the primary field of pain, this *knowing* is foreign to the body and mind. It requires a leap of faith into the Mystery of all things, to begin to *believe* a core truth that is in fact your birthright.

First, you must understand that the field of pain you were born into is not yours – it is not personal. Although you had a personal experience of the events that have unfolded throughout your life and you might even be convinced that you were partially responsible for some of it, the truth is that you could not change your circumstances until you had the agency (personal power) to do so.

The agency I am referring to usually is available once our brain is fully developed around the age of 24, according to Dr. Dan Siegel.[6] However, we could argue that for some of us, we discovered personal power during the late teen years. At birth the brain is a sponge, absorbing everything in its external environments to make sense of life on earth. During the first two years of life, our brain is learning how to think, feel, and behave as a human. Hence, we are imprinted by our primary environment. How they think, feel, and behave informs our system.

As a toddler we begin to differentiate. At this stage, we notice 'I' is separate from 'them'. Along with these changes in perception, our brain is moving through differing brain wave patterns. As

---

[6] Siegel, D. (2013). *Brainstorm: The Power and Purpose of the Teenage Brain*. New York: Tarcher/Penguin.; Siegel, D. (2017). *Mind: A Journey to the Heart of Being Human*. New York: W.W. Norton & Company.

a toddler we have moved from Delta – slow and wide-open consciousness – to Theta. In Theta it is noted that we are receptive to deep programming and healing. It is a slow meditative expansive, and imaginal brain wave state. After which, as an adolescent we engage in the imaginal realm with Alpha brain wave frequencies being the dominant state. Not until age twelve do we shift into the familiar brain wave pattern of Beta. Beta waves are experienced as rational, focused, linear, and analytic states. For the most part we hang out in Beta day-to-day.

If we receive our program during delta and theta stages of development, it is argued that to change the pattern we must return to those altered states of consciousness. Hence, talk therapy is often not enough to change our imprint.

What gives rise to an altered state of consciousness?

There are many ways to engage the altered state that are not drug induced. The primary tool that costs nothing, except time, is meditation. However, movement like ecstatic dance, yoga, or running moves you into a flow state, expanding awareness and shifting you out of Beta states. Certain hypnosis techniques can move you into hypnagogic states. Prayer and chanting are ancient acts for such a practice. Ceremony and ritual are used to engage altered states. Creative expression is another way of moving out of Beta and into Alpha.

However, tapping into the altered state of brain wave patterns is not enough to change the program. There is an act of will that is required of you. And, part of the process is clearing out all of the trapped emotional material that has been accumulated over the years. This undigested emotional debris is waiting to be felt and here in lies the problem that so many people experience at this stage of the journey – **they are afraid to feel too much, for too long**.

If we have never been shown how to feel our emotions without becoming consumed by them, than it makes perfect sense why so many humans are terrified to go inside and sift through this debris. One emotional outburst could result in an interior tsunami in which the system perceives danger.

Riding Your Emotions

We are so afraid of our emotions.

Afraid to feel them. Granted, for many, there are good reasons for resisting 'feeling the feelings'. For example, feeling and emoting usually resulted in punishment or negative consequences in our past and most likely, did not change the circumstances.

Take my soulmate for example, as he recounts about his childhood, that was full of adversity and trauma. He learned very young that crying or feeling the pain of it did not change the circumstances, it made the pain worse. He continued to report that he 'stopped feeling the feelings'. It has taken him close to 40 years to learn how to feel again.

Feeling=unsafe=more pain

With such an equation it makes sense why a person would shut down their capacity to feel, period. Why would anyone want to encourage feeling the 'feelings' as a form of healing when the past tells you that feeling anything is too painful and potential life threatening?

For many we learned very young that if I feel what I am feeling in my body, I might die or go crazy; I might explode in pain or be met with more pain. Considering the fact that our biological system's primary motivation is to keep us safe, it makes sense why the system would shut down the capacity to feel as a form of protection.

Few of us were taught how to 'be with' the feelings and sensations arising in the body. Further, few of us were shown how to move the emotions through our system without become attached to them. And finally, few of us were met with presence, attuned attention, and caring connection from our primary caregivers to help us integrate, tolerate, and understand what we were feeling.

As children we need caregivers who can help us make sense out of huge emotional charges felt in our bodies and teach us how to move that energy without causing harm to self or others. In order for this to occur, the caregiver must know themselves what to do with highly charged emotional information in their own systems. This requires a kind of awakening on their part.

Therefore, a huge part of therapy and healing is focused on tolerating big sensations and uncomfortable emotions within each person's system. Taking into account that a large proportion of people do not like to feel painful emotions like grief, sadness, anger, remorse, terror, and fear.

We are living in a confusing time because on one hand we are encouraged to feel, but we are told that if we feel too much that there is something wrong with us. We are told to feel more, and yet, we are not taught how to be with the emotions as they arise.

How do we change this perspective and build trust in the process of feeling?

Trauma therapy emphasizes the need for safety – emotional safety. There is a lot of consideration and time invested in helping the client learn how to shift states – move out of discomfort – and build capacity to tolerate more discomfort without feeling out of control. Dan Siegel calls this your Window of Tolerance.[7] The capacity that you have to tolerate stressful information in the form of thoughts, sensations, feelings, and images.

The idea is that we are born with a set window of tolerance and childhood experiences and environment either strengthen or weaken this system. It is suggested that we can expand or widen our window of tolerance to be able to hold more stressful information without becoming dysregulated. One of the main tools that helps with this is integrating a mindful awareness

---

[7] Siegel, D. (2018). *Aware: The Science and Practice of Presence.* Melbourne: Scribe Publications.

practice into your daily life.

Foundationally, we need to re-program the system (i.e., body and mind) that it is safe and normal to feel. And that the system can handle emotional stress without causing damage. If we have no map for feeling, how do we expect to open to feeling the emotions?

If the current reality is such that any activated felt sensation in the body, any uncomfortable emotion or any dysregulation equals danger, then it will be difficult to shift out of your current struggles. We effort to block, shut down, or dissociate for relief and comfort. You know the term comfortably numb; this is familiar for many.

From this perspective, feeling is perceived as harmful and outside of one's control. This is the key statement – perceived as outside of your control. Many think that emotions are happening to them without their control or permission. Therefore, if they have no control over their feelings and emotions, how are they supposed to change anything, or do anything about it?

This perception lends to learned helplessness; victims to our emotional reality. As if emotions are wildfires in our system that came out of nowhere and are running wild.

The only control we perceive is to stop it before it

happens, or block it. Otherwise, we are perceiving our experience as totally outside of our control – a runaway freight train.

This perception keeps us stuck in a fear response:

Perceived fear = constriction and tension = pain = panic.

Thus, the habitual answer is to feel less, not more. Is it any wonder why we do everything in our power to numb out?

The problem is that remaining comfortably numb wreaks havoc on our mood and relationships. We feel lifeless, depressed, uneasy, discouraged, distant, distracted, disoriented, empty. Some of us feel the opposite: too jacked up, hypervigilant, overly controlling, anxious, always on the go, critical, and striving for perfection. Beneath both of these examples exists a deep dissatisfaction in life and a chronic insecurity that if felt, which is terrifying and destabilizing.

Again, why would anyone want to feel this core insecurity?

Did you know that both ecstasy and fear generate the same chemicals? The difference is the perception. Both produce adrenaline followed by endorphins. One is for pleasure and one is to avoid pain.

The new possibility is to *feel* more.

But what if feeling more leads to dysregulation and harm? What is dysregulation? And why are we (therapists) so focused on it? Simply stated, dysregulation is the body's way of indicating that it has popped out of its 'window of tolerance'. In other words, it is your body's way of communicating with you that it is not handling the stressful information very well; it is alerting you as a warning signal. How much stressful information we can handle before we move into a dysregulated state, is unique to each individual.

We all experience dysregulation of our energy and emotional system. The key is recognizing the signs and symptoms of such an experience and noting that it is information first and foremost. The brain is a meaning making machine and seeks to make sense out of moment-to- moment experiences, which is both a blessing and a hindrance. Often, without conscious awareness, humans impose meaning (make up a narrative) onto the felt sensations of dysregulation. For example: These feelings mean I am unsafe; This sensation means I am about to have a panic attack; These body feelings mean danger.

When we do this without conscious awareness, we move away from the felt sensation and emotional expression and attune our attention on the narrative or thought. Thus, we get carried away with the perception of what is happening in our bodies and what it means and find ourselves in a state of more discomfort.

We need to learn or re-learn how to feel. We need to learn what to do with the emotional information that we experience in the body. We need to trust that our body can handle highly charged emotional information and can process it without exploding or going crazy.

I invite you to consider a new belief: You are bigger, more powerful, greater than your emotions, your body and your past.

Journal Entry

The child is tired. She is tired of carrying the burden. The *Mother Wound*. She screams out 'no more', angry and irritated. The burden consumed by the pain. Open and sensitive to the surroundings. Wearing her nervous system on her skin, but of course her nervous system is on her skin. The skin the largest organ of the body. The vessel – receiving all that is in her immediate environment. Grief. That was in the environment; her mother's grief. The *Mother's* grief. I'll take it and hold it in my soul vessel. Survival instinct they say. Must hold the burden, must break the pain, must take it on. In hope of re-connecting to The *Mother*; the wounded mother. It was not her fault. She wears the scars well, covered up in success. 'I must take it on,' she says. 'I must do something with it all,' she says. 'I must take it away, the suffering,' she says. 'If only I can take it all away, I could connect to the nectar once again.' Take on more, take it away. On and on she goes until she it fat and bloated with the *Mother Wound*. Can't contain anymore, can't do it anymore. She bursts as her vessel overflows with unwept tears; so many tears, all bleeding together in one big cosmic soup. Can't differentiate whose tears are who's anymore. No more. She tempers. Not one more ounce of suffering can enter this vessel. First identify the burden. What is contained in the vessel as burdensome? She believed it was her duty to tend to the *Mother Wound*; Her responsibility to take *it* away. The suffering, to ease the pain. She couldn't take it away. The great ultimate failure. She has failed. She couldn't take it away. She believed with all her Being that she could take it away. And only at that point would she feel free to be alive and to be a child. The work is not done until all the suffering ends and is alleviated. Until then, She, the girl, will forever suffer. I see, in the horizon, a clearing, a liberation. Freedom from the curse – the great curse. What is a curse? And what frees one from a curse? If the Girl cannot alleviate the suffering of the *Mother*, who will? And who can? Who, what, does she pass on the suffering and pour out the pain from her vessel? I wailed and wailed for what felt like centuries during my medicine journey. Was this wailing emptying the vessel?

ANGER

First there was shock.
There was denial.
Anger crept in through the back door.

Blue cold anger
Red hot anger
Brewing and bubbling.

All in an attempt to keep grief at the door.
Fucking grief – both friend and foe
Medicine for the soul
Unwelcomed medicine.

To walk with grief
And through it
Can feel like you've been bathed by a waterfall.

Letting go to let grief in
is not an easy task
Reminds me of the lyrics
it hurts so good.

Why don't I want to grieve?

My child is not okay

She is having a temper tantrum
She doesn't like death.
Who likes death anyway?

Non-attachment bullshit
Pseudo name for
shut-down-psychopath
Numb; comfortably numb.

That is what *that* is.

I'll find my way.
I always do.
But for now
I'm stuck in anger.

Voices from Within

There are many voices communicating with us internally. Naming them and hearing what they are saying, questioning them, and choosing which ones are worthy of listening to is an important step in the healing process. Working to differentiate all the inner players has proven to be extremely beneficial, albeit hard. One of my mentors, Bonnie Badenoch, calls this our inner community. I like this notion – inner community. The invitation is to summon all the players to the table. Not one part is to be left out or banished.

One of my parts was the inner voice of destruction. The thought of inviting her to the inner table bothered me. I didn't like her, nor did I want her to be included. I preferred the notion of destroying her, getting rid of her, banishing her for ever. Her purpose was to destroy my sense of worth, so I believed. Why would I want to bring her closer? Why would anyone want to make friends with their inner demons?

I can recall viscerally the moment it shifted for me. Bonnie invited me to consider how the voice of inner destruction came about? How was she born; under what circumstances? I was reminded that

all these parts – good and bad – have played an
important role in our existence. They are always
working *for* us, not against us. Even when it feels
like these parts are trying to devastate. I am told
they are all working to keep you safe – to protect
you.

My inner voice of destruction was trying to keep
me safe. This sounded preposterous and non-
logical. She fed my shame and paralyzed me,
she drained me of my life force. How in the hell
is she protecting me? It would appear that she
was destroying me. I learned to still my mind and
leaned into my inner landscape to listen to what
she had to say. Fuck me, Bonnie was right. I could
see, rather, know that this character was born out
of intense pain. In fact, she had no agenda to harm.
Her desire has always been to help move the pain.
Whoa. What does that mean or look like? I asked.

In time I could see that she was responding to
the pent-up interior soul-pain. This pain needed
to move; be removed. I understood (without
thinking) that when we endure a great amount
of soul-pain and we have not been taught how to
move it through and out of our system, we need a
way to discharge the pain. The pain cannot remain
stagnant; it is constantly in motion. When there
is a large amount of internalized pain with no exit,
the voice of destruction is born. If the pain cannot
be externalized, it is internalized. It is absorbed

within the psyche in the form of inner abuse. The voice of destruction is the voice of abuse. If this is true, why would I want to invite my inner abuser to sit at my table?

The role she is playing – my inner abuser – is the only role she knows how to play. She is trying to move the energy of pain out of my system in the only way she knows how – to inflict pain.

The pain was too much for a child to carry, and so it was swallowed and projected into my interior world. Her role has always been to help me feel that which I was afraid to feel. She kept me alive in this way. Even though her voice could be loud at times (and cruel), she still kept me alive. The trick is to stop believing what she is saying and to start *feeling* what she had been rearranging for eons – the inner pain. The voice of destruction, the inner abuser, was a shapeshifter. A master of energy manipulation. Look, I am not suggesting we celebrate our inner abuser voice (or the outer abusers in our lives), but the deeper we go into the possibility that everything is actually working in our favour (not against us) we might be able to stop the wheel of suffering.

And, this is exactly what I did. I befriended my inner abuser. Eventually, I could love her and furthermore, thank her. The closer I sat with her, the more I learned about her role. As I learned to move the energy of pain throughout my system, and discharge the pent-up emotional material, the voice of destruction silenced. For those of you who have lived with an inner abuser, you know how horrendous and relentless it is. The quietening of this inner voice is heaven on earth. There is a difference between the silencing and *silencing*. I am not referring to further separation and suppression here, I am truly expressing the diminishing power of this voice. She no longer had a role. The pain was moving, and space was being created within, thus, the voice of destruction could settle down. And that is exactly what she did.

I did not banish her, I thanked her. In fact, I fell in love with her. Love heals, period. In all of this, I understood what Bonnie was talking about when she said, 'all are welcome at the table'. Even the greatest of inner evils, is welcome. Embodiment can only be experienced when we are whole; whole because every part has been loved. This great observation resulted in the end of self-destructive behaviour, self-harm, self-hatred, and misery. It wasn't replaced with positive self-talk; it was replaced with *Love*.

Byron Katie and her powerful tool called The Work, is beneficial in deconstructing the internal stressful dialogue that is constantly on chatter mode. Using what she refers to as the 4 questions and a turnaround, you can very simply and powerfully learn how to quiet the mind and experience peace. I recommend using a few different 'modalities' to help with this area of healing. The Integral Institute and Genpo Rochi, refer to something called The Big Mind. This is another 'technique' teaching the principle of mind parts, ego parts, or voices within. Learning to identify them, personify them, and then, be in relationship with them is a proven method for healing the mind chaos.

I personally, have spent over ten years reading, listening to, and applying the life teachings of Caroline Myss, she offers grounded and real spiritual teachings. Her work on archetypes is some of the best I have read. Furthermore, she has a dynamic way of delivering information about the human energy body, providing insight into the world of both physical and spiritual.

When referring to self-parts or voices from within, there are many, and they all have a powerful effect on your core belief system. For example, usually there are tribal (ancient) voices, cultural voices, ego voices, soul voices and many more. It is helpful to pay attention to which voices hold the most power? Which ones do you hear most often? Which ones dominate your internal world?

Name them.
What are they saying?
Speak to them from your interior soul voice. Describe them in best detail.

When you listen to them, how do you feel?
Write about who you were.
Write about who you are right now.
Write about who you want to become.

And if your interior landscape has an entire community of parts and players, where are *You* in the mix? *Who* are you? *What* are you? Where do you rest at the table? *Are you merely the composition of all the parts*? Or are you the Watcher? The Conductor?

For years I lived dominated by the voice of the destroyer - my critic, my controller, and my guilt(er). There are many more parts, however, and these caused the greatest damage.

Recognizing this has been very empowering because I now have the ability to see clearly, which part is driving my life. When I was shut down, I felt as if I had no control over who was in charge. I was clearly not in the driver's seat; I was asleep at the wheel. My programmed inner parts, born out life's adversities, were running the show. In fact, they were in the creation of my life. Identifying them, naming them, understanding them, and eventually loving them, has been a core part of my healing. The process of mind excavation takes courage, indeed. However, the great collapse removes the option to remain asleep. Navigating the interior terrain includes dancing with your demons. Eventually, transforming them.

THE HEALER

Enslaved to the demands of the suffering
They come in droves,
Kneeling down in front of
Her.

Defeated and deflated
Continuing to pour out
No tap to turn off
Healing energy flowing through *Her*
A river.

She is shrinking in exhaustion
Her purpose
The suffering and the pain
Is endless.

An endless stream of suffering
Never ending until *She* ends
To only do it all over again.
The soul knows to heal
But at what cost?

The task Master demanding
She is of service
Relentlessly, to give and keep giving

From the endless well of healing
Energy.

But the body can't keep up
Fading away into a shadow
Of a self.
The love is strong
But the light is dim.

Who is in charge?
Who turns off the tap?
Who feeds *Her?*
You are enslaved to the wrong God
She says.

Journal Entry

A baby is shaking in a convulsion-like force. It is nauseating; I am nauseous. An image of being smashed in the back by a Cosmic Hand and **crows flying out of my mouth** *– lots of them. My mouth opens wide and a sense of singing truth overwhelms me. I cry. My voice is used as an instrument for inspiration. My message matters.*

SOUL SPEAK

I'd rather speak to your soul
than try to please your personality.

Soul-speak awakes that which has been dormant
buried deep within the *womb* well.

Soul-voice is wrought with gritty contradictions and
words that make you cringe.

Words we don't want to hear.

I often wonder if it's best to remain silent,
to remain asleep.

I'm reminded of this truth every time I look at a
perfectly poised and manicured 'life is grand' picture on
Instagram followed by 400 comments and 23k likes.

We want eye candy and pseudo soul.
We want inspiration neatly tied with a ribbon.
We want anything that does not require *work*.

I'm just bitter sometimes
bitter that I can't help but speak from my soul.

#ijustwanttobefamousoninstagram

PART TWO
INSTINCTIVE *Birth* AS A METAPHOR

"*I saw birth proceed without anyone managing or directing it. I call this pattern the Holistic Stages of Labor and while I recognize that each woman gives birth individually, a specific overarching pattern emerged that was perceptible in each labor. The language I have chosen to describe these stages befits a journey, a rite of passage or a sacred event rather than a medical process. It is symbolic and poetic rather than clinical although this does not imply that the process I have witnessed is a metaphor for labor.* **What I have seen is actual and tangible, totally discernible**." ~ Whapio

A Soul Birth

I want to preface this section with an important question to hold: Why would you, or anyone, want to give birth to this new version of Soul-Self? For what purpose?

The concern I have as I write about the excavation of our interior landscape, in hopes to come home to our Soul, is that it is being driven by the greatest deception of all time – human supremacy. The insidiousness of this core human assumption and imprint exists in all of us – it has to, it *is* the water we swim in. If the desire to awaken is driven from the invisible drive to arrive as the ultimate supreme human, superior to all living organisms (including nature) then you have missed the mark. Big time.

And, my fear is that a large part of the spiritual industry is in fact, poisoned by the curse of human supremacy. Using this core point of view to influence people to gain more power – spiritual power – to continue to feed the *Great Beast*.

Allow me to elaborate. The self-absorbed drive to heal, to resolve the inner anguish, has the potential to awaken you to your true nature. And, from my vantage point, our true nature is humble. It can *see* that its only point is to attune to Life itself. It understands that it is actually unimportant, yet one with all that is, thus incredibly important. A paradox indeed.

It finds its place in the great Mystery of Life. And perhaps, for the first time ever, can question the possibility that *it* doesn't know...anything. And in the not knowing, it doesn't matter. From this gentle place of presence, *it* (Soul) can show up in relation to the natural world. There is a simplicity in the awakened Soul. I wonder if you knew that what was on the other side of the sleeping dragon, was a very mundane vibrant sense of reality, if you would continue to work so hard? Nothing grandiose; nothing special. In fact, your sense of specialness dissolves in the process. Fuck, the ego does not like to *not* be special. How else can human supremacy live?

The question remains: What will you do with the newfound power that resides within?

As I have come to see it, **a soul birth is a dynamic experience of inner transformation**. When you take the plunge to consciously venture into the dark night of the soul, and find your way out of the inner chaos, what can emerge is the greatest gift of all: to finally stop being at war with Life itself. However, as with birth, there are no guarantees. Albeit, awakening is our birthright, as is instinctive birthing, and yet, there are still unknown factors that keep the journey in the realm of the Mystery.

You begin, with the great fall - a life catalyst - and start your descent into the world of pain and darkness. Thus, the emotional contractions mark the beginning of your labor. Along the way, while in the tunnel of despair, baring the weight of your grief and wrestling with your inner demons, you discover an internal fire to birth yourself anew. Thus, giving birth to your Soul-self.

Indeed, this is a Soul-directed process of becoming undone and facing the internal chaos that lives within your interior landscape and causes anguish of the mind. You must traverse the mind-field before passing through the gate of the Soul. And, do not be mistaken, there is a death. Some of us get trapped in the underworld, gripped by the horrors of the mind movies. Labor is hard work, period. And laboring to awaken to your true nature, your soul nature, is equally if not more taxing. In the end, everyone (who chooses to proceed) navigates this terrain differently, just as every woman in labor follows her labor individually.

Your soul-birth is unique to you.

To live is to grow; morph. I am reminded of what Elizabeth Kubler-Ross had to say about this notion, "Everyone goes through hardship in life. The more you go through the more you grow... and [I] believe that our only purpose for existing is to grow."[8] A labor is experienced along this path of evolution (potentially many labors); how you navigate is up to you. It is recommended that you experience your inner chaos fully, consciously, and with inner sight. Use your emotional labor pains as an opportunity to face that which terrifies you, trusting that in the end you will come out whole and *alive*. In this wholeness, lives great peace and purpose. And although you already embody all of this, closing the gap leads to this interior peace.

There are many spiritual truths that guide during these hard times. It is asked of you to draw upon them, for nothing within the human mind realm can provide you with the strength, courage, and power necessary to overcome your soul pain. It is of no surprise that I found comfort and truth in the wisdom of instinctive birth as a spiritual path.

During an instinctive labor, **there is an internal blueprint guiding the way**.

A woman carries physiological knowledge that knows how to give birth. The growing baby also has imprinted within its system a knowing as to how to navigate its own labor. The problem has been that modern technology and minds have meddled with this instinctive process due to fear

---

[8] Kubler-Ross, E. (2005). **On Grief and Grieving**. New York: Scribner.

and a need to control; and herein lies the discord between the innate wisdom and ancient truths about birth.

The fear-based belief systems have imprinted the minds of many. Resulting in behaviours that intervene and control the instinctive process. With this in mind, trust is severed. If we are never given the opportunity to know and experience the incredible Wisdom that resides within our biological and energetic system, how are we to surrender in trust? And yet, trust is the medicine and the antidote to settle the fear.

As noted, fear and technological advancements are the cause of much of the disconnection between these two worlds – instinctive responses versus rational minds. Birth cannot unfold instinctively while in the rational mind. Birth is a primal experience, which means instinctive. When we labor, we use the ancient, primal, oldest part of our brain, the reptilian survival brain.

Nothing is rational about giving birth and nothing is rational about inner transformation.

French Obstetrician, Dr. Michel Odent, author and founder of the primal health research data bank has dedicated his entire career to researching and disseminating knowledge about the instinctive processes of childbirth. He has this to say in regard to the brain:

"While our upper brain, our neocortex, handles the information given to it by the sense organs and is able to have knowledge of the universe which is limited by time and space, the primal brain goes beyond that, beyond the rational world. Life has been able to develop, evolve, and get more complex because the supercomputer contained in the new brain has been at its service. But from the moment this supercomputer becomes over powerful and represses the primal brain the whole of life will be threatened."[9]

If the above statement is true, that the neocortex is becoming too powerful and in control, then we may be thwarting the instinctive nature of *being* human: being *alive*. As humans, we cannot solely exist in the rational brain; the left hemisphere. For optimum health, the brain must flow through altered states of consciousness throughout the day, sleep being our primary engagement of altered states, in which we move between hemispheres and through all brain wave frequencies (beta, alpha, theta, delta).

Ancient cultures have known this, if not rationally, then instinctively. The rituals of their cultures, religions, ceremonies, and gatherings demonstrate this. These events were necessary to create an outlet for the 'group' to tap into their primal

---

[9] Odent, M. (2002). **Primal Health**. East Sussex: Clairview Books.

brains. Often medicinal plants, dancing, singing, trance drumming, heat (sweat lodges), fasting, and body piercing were all used as a means to induce an altered state of consciousness. In turn, silencing the rational mind and connecting with the expanded Mind.

In return, communities would experience healings, find answers to questions and problems, commune with nature, and discover a deeper trust in the Great Mystery. Of course, these choices and acts were not consciously chosen because they 'activate the primal brain and the pineal gland', rather they were cultural customs that assisted in the health of community and fostered connection.

Currently, some neuroscientists are researching something called the 'God part of the brain' to further understand mystical experiences, transpersonal realities, and the power of prayer and healing. Modern researcher Matthew Alper, in his works *The God Part of The Brain*, supports the above thoughts with the following words:

"Besides engaging in such practices as prayer, chant, dance, yoga, or meditation, many world cultures have used psychedelic drugs as yet another means through which to evoke a mystical experience... apparently, by focusing our attentions on what we perceive as the transcendent, that is, by praying (or meditating) – our species has the capacity to alter our physiologies in such a way that we can reduce stress levels, prompting a chain of healing responses upon the body."[10]

It's interesting to note that today's modern culture (especially counter-culture groups) is still finding ways to tap into this instinctive knowledge. Today, there is a modern resurgence in body art, piercing, electronic dance, and 'medicinal' drug induced altered states. As modern culture replaces these ancient rituals with technological advancements and industrialization, it is of no coincidence that we will continue to seek experiences that tap us into these ancient and very human, primal states of being in which the ego-self dissolves and the wild creature emerges.

Mentors, Shamans, and Medicine Women have told me that healing happens in altered states of consciousness: *behind the veil of waking reality*. This notion aligns with the truth of instinctive birthing. Humans induce the altered state while sleeping, creatively expressing, singing, meditating, journeying, praying, laughing, orgasming, dancing to name a few.

Therefore, you cannot make nor force healing to

---

[10] Alper, M. (2008). **The "God" Part of the Brain: A Scientific Interpretation of Human Spirituality and God.** Naperville: Sourcebook Inc.

happen; rather, you must allow yourself to *receive* the healing. In the same ways that in birth, you *receive* the light of the newborn: *Dar La Luz*.

Perhaps, giving birth to one's Soul, is to receive *your* light?

If the above is true, which based on research and my own experiences is verifying to be the case, then I suggest that there is a similarity between both the world of instinctive childbirth and that of the interior work of transformation. As previously stated, I liken this journey of transformation to a Soul birth. Under this assumption, the notion that there is purpose in the chaos of life holds merit, as there is purpose in the chaos of birth. The chaos is a necessary component for growth; pushing you through the discomfort. This annoying brutal discomfort initiates the fires of change, as with the onset of labour pains.

An initiation is essential in the great waking up.

As I speak about purposeful chaos, I can't help but to ponder the question: What is the difference between organized chaos and that of calamity? Where is the fine line between the two? At what point is the chaos dangerous rather than purposeful? How might someone *know* the difference? These are important questions to consider. They are important because organized chaos is productive whereas, calamity triggers the survival response.

Bottom line: **You cannot give birth when your survival response is activated.**

Though, the more we intervein with life's chaos in attempts to reduce its intensity, we thwart the instinctive process of healing. During childbirth, interruptions can lead to complicated births, disempowered experiences, and an increase in mortality rates.[11] In other words, meddling in the chaos is potentially dangerous and a powerful inhibitor of the process. And yet, in pain, we want to find ways to take it all away; we often want someone or something to disturb the process. To control or take charge of the experience that is unfolding. On one hand, instinctively we want to move away from the pain, not be in relationship with it. On the other hand, I am suggesting that we override this drive to give rise to a deeper initiation by *leaning* into the chaos.

Childbirth is a prime example of purposeful pain in which women in labour are encouraged to *surrender* to the pain. This notion can be viewed as a contradiction. Many women have had to learn to disembody in pain as a form of survival. To suggest that you/they relax *into* the pain can be experienced as preposterous. Remember that

---

[11] Odent, M. (1984). **Birth Reborn**. New York: Pantheon.

trauma severs the cord of trust; fractures you
from your body and soul. And thus, if a mother
in labour learned very early in life that pain
meant harm to the body and soul, there is little
opportunity to have learned how to surrender to
purposeful pain. In fact, it is absolutely possible that
for such a woman, no concept of purposeful pain
exists as a potential truth. As such, a mother is apt
to dissociate as a form of protection in response to
even the smallest amount of potential pain; birth is
full of potential pain.

Here in lies a familiar conflict: If a mother has
never learned to trust in purposeful pain, how
is she going to *surrender* to the pains of labour?
Everything in her body is going to resist this notion
with the onset of labor pain. The same potential
conflict possibly exists for you, in that, how are you
going to *surrender* in trust to life's *purposeful* pain if
you are only familiar with harmful pain? To discern
between these two pain points – purposeful or
harmful pain- is a critical juncture within your
passage. You (and the mother) are being nudged
to *lean in* towards the pain once you have clearly
differentiated between the two types of pain.

I am asking you to consider these new
perspectives associated with pain, chaos, and
transformation in attempts to arouse purpose
in preparation for the arduous healing journey
ahead. True, I am suggesting that the purposeful

pain and chaos in your life is a necessary ingredient for healing and transformation. And the meddling, halting, numbing, and fearing the pain is prolonging the process. The invitation is to *lean into* its intensity and allow the instinctive process to unfold in all its wildness. In the end, creating internal space; so much spaciousness. Transformation unfolds in this expanded state of space. The space that exists between the colliding particles, that create form. Possibility is *alive* in the field of spaciousness. And, this quality of spaciousness I speak about is unattainable when in a survival response. Thus, as with any transformative journey, mapping out the territory is essential.

There is a way and an art in 'reading' the field of labor and birth. Unfortunately, modern day teachings do not teach this art. As with modern medicine, we have lost the art to 'train' healers, rather we train Doctors and caregivers to fear nature itself. During a labor, there are marking points (stages and spirals) that assist in the process and encourage the mother to keep on going. These guiding truths about labor and birth are what I have used to find my way through the foreign terrain of grief, despair, and death.

These are the spiritual truths I am about to reveal to you to hopefully sooth the voice of fear.

Instinctive birth keepers of the old and new

(rebellious peoples) have imparted their knowledge and truths about birth throughout the time. These wise people have much to say about the truths of birth and transformation. Their knowledge, gathered from collectively witnessing thousands of women find their power in labor, offers information about the challenge's and triumphs women face in childbirth. They also offer a powerful symbolic lens to understand the journey of healing.

Throughout the years I have garnered wisdom from this school of thought, accumulating well over 10,000 hours of study of instinctive physiological childbirth. It is possible that at this stage of modern evolution and advancements, that very few childbearing families and caregivers will ever *know* instinctive birth. It may in fact become a myth: *A traditional story, especially one concerning the early history of a people or explaining some natural or social phenomenon, and typically involving supernatural beings or events.*[12]

Similar to the process of birth, much about grief is detached from everyday conversation. Rarely are we taught how to grieve. This, in my opinion, is a dangerous truth. The ramifications of not properly grieving are atrocious, and this can be

---

[12] Oxford Dictionary. (2019). Retrieved from http://english.oxford-dictionaries.com/myth.

seen every day via internet, news, radio, war, TV, the plethora of violence, over prescription of psychopharmaceuticals, and rising rates of suicide. Learning how to navigate the grief waters, without disembodying, is akin to riding the waves of contractions during childbirth; staying connected to the sensations with utmost presence.

Each contraction - each wave of grief - engulfs the body filling it with foreign (yet soulfully familiar) sensations. These overwhelming sensations are experienced by the mind, heart and body. Resulting in an internal judgement or assessment of such. Depending on our imprinted past, the sensations are understood as either dangerous or safe. If feeling too much was followed by harm or further pain, it makes sense that in the current pain of grief, there would be fear. If, however, feeling too much was met with encouragement and compassion, and understood as a form of discharging emotional debris, there would be trust. Trust is rare. Thus, we need to re-learn and re-member ourselves home. And, for many, we need a metaphor, a story, or a map to settle the mind. Ultimately, we are being encouraged to *believe* in a new potential: The pain that I am experiencing is *not* dangerous but rather, safe.

During labor, the end in sight is the peak experience of giving birth to a newborn. During your Soul's birth, your endpoint is the peak experience of actively pulling yourself out of the trenches and becoming enchanted by your internal power.

You become the sovereign human of your life.

Everything you thought you were is no longer true. All that you were and all that you attached identity to has died along the way, and something new has emerged. Such a journey requires courage, compassion, love, endurance, determination, stamina, support and spiritual purpose.

Part of the soul birthing process is the action applied to the keen excavation of your interior world and inquisition of your mind. As you come face to face with that which frightens you, hurts you, tears you apart, and rips out your insides; you have no choice but to battle those voices of the underworld; eventually flowing with grace into the heart of the pain. The metaphor I am applying is an encouraging way (albeit hard) to engage life's worst challenges.

ODE TO THE WOMB

Blood Moon
Pregnant and full
Alive and vibrant
Unified in the mysterious,
Terrifying in her power.

Bleed, dam it, release
Wash over us and cleanse
Purifying in your blood.

Red moon
Womb moon
Rich moon
Holding creation
Containing truth.

Ode to the
      Beautiful
           Bleeding
                  Heart

Sacred moon
Sovereign moon
Tending to the flow
The tides, the ebbs
Majestic in form and glow.

She who dances
In the night sky
Bless *Her*
Bless you.

Journal Entry

What was I anchoring in?
Breath.

Where did I go?

Traversed many lands through portals. Journeyed
to the spirit world. Tobacco carried me there
sacred medicine. Ancient love. Helper. Guide.
Form dissolved; consciousness remained. Body as
a vessel, holding Life force.

There is room for all of it.

Spaciousness – that is what we are doing. Making
space. Every mother needs to make space. We are
a portal for Spirit to come through; for Life to take
form.

I get it.

Music takes us there. Spirit shows us many forms
and faces. It is all God; it is all Sacred. The energy
behind the mind; behind the story; behind the
personality. Unity. Space. More and more space.
Expanding beyond many limits. We do ritual to
keep the thread alive, so it doesn't go dormant. We

communicate with the Spirit realm through this thread; through sound. And, through smell and tears. We/Consciousness flows along those cords of energy. There are many cords and we can get distracted. And sound, presence, tobacco guide us. They direct us to Source.

Opening to let God in...

The ancient wise woman braiding. Braids. Owls. Jaguars. Eagles. Snakes – lots of snakes. Creature – I turned into my creature. Energy held within energy. Infinite energy. So, Love full.

Quantum Midwifery AS A METAPHOR FOR HEALERS AND CARETAKERS

"We need to promote and protect normal birth simply because the future of humanity depends on it. Our ability to love is nurtured in the womb...As midwives [of the soul] we carry a huge responsibility to disseminate this knowledge... Midwives who understand the importance of not disturbing normal physiology and who work to protect undisturbed birth are the true guardians of the birth territory." ~ Kathleen Fahy

Navigating Your Soul's Birth

Each labor takes on a soul of its own. There is a dance that is happening, a spiral dance, as the mother spirals deeper into her labor. This encourages her to become undone in the process, as she surrenders deeper to the flow. Along the way, when left to her own devices, the Mother finds her internal power and courage to give birth to her baby. This power I speak about is the end result of having faced the fears, doubts, insecurities, and imprints that have kept the small self under the spell of safety. There is newfound trust in the unknown. Some call this quality of trust, faith.

Childbirth is not a linear journey, as the patriarchal medical view would have us believe, but rather a journey of unknowns. A woman's cervix does not simply dilate from 0 cm to 10 cm and then birth a baby through stages and phases of labor; there is far more occurring than physical measurements.

There is a cellular morphing happening, and a *death*. **The maiden is dying**. New life is born with the birth of a baby; as well as **the birth of the mother**.

We forget the latter, with so much of the attention on the birth of the baby at *all* cost. The birth of the Mother is ignored, devalued, and at times, dismembered. She does not matter. This truth was the grit behind my Healing After Birth manuscript and program, in which I brought voice to the ignored Mother through the journey of birth; the wounded Mother.

How can you claim your newborn if you, as the Mother, have been dehumanized along the way?

What happens from conception onwards is a demonstration of human potential and sacred magic. There is a biological process of unfolding that occurs during this time. This process expands in depth and breadth, and it is the dance of labor. Although, with a Soul birth, you may have no idea *what* is being born or how the soul journey will feel, I hope you are beginning to trust in the described process and the internal madness. This is a process of metamorphosis. A part of you is dissolving and dying, and it must.

You must get out of the way in order for you to experience your birth. Who and what is the *You* that is being asked to 'get out of the way'? Some call this your ego, small-self, perception of self, human-self.

Regardless of what you call the *You* that is dying, there is a death that comes before the birth.

What is dying? Who is dying? What needs to die? Let us look at this dance of labor so you can identify where you might be within your own life labor. Before we start, take a moment to ponder what I mean by the term 'life labor'. What does this look like in your experience? What were the catalysts? What desires to be born? What is your soul saying? To whom is your soul speaking?

One might say that we are always in a labor of some sort, always growing and evolving, ebbing and flowing, pushing and pulling, opening and closing, expanding and contracting, tensing and releasing; life is full of stress, on purpose. It is of no accident that life spirals as it does, and that we are flooded with experiences that challenge us, for great discomfort call us to attention.

From this viewpoint, I keep reiterating the need to let life's labor carry you away, trusting that there is inherent wisdom within your system that knows the terrain of *birth* (soul birth). This requires a belief in the concept of awakening; of waking up. With trust and a belief in such a notion, the labor pains can transport you to a realm that exists behind the veil; to bring forth new life. There are, however, some important recommendations that support instinctive birthing to unfold. As such, it is suggested that a laboring woman's environment include the following[13]

---

[13] Buckley, S. (2015). *Hormonal Physiology of Childbearing: Evidence*

- She feels safe and secure
- She feels loved and nurtured
- She feels free from confinements and be liberated to move as needed
- She is warm and has access to dim lighting
- She has agency to make informed decisions
- She feels private and protected
- There is little to no interruption – no intrusive talking or watching
- She is encouraged, with no authority figure telling her what to do
- She has a trust in her body and the process of birth
- She has access to a wise, knowledgeable, trustworthy guardian of birth

I am suggesting that these are the same key ingredients to move through the spiritual labor process. You are intrinsically coded to heal; this knowledge is held within the cells of your body and soul. Your path of awakening and transformation, is therefore, already encrypted within the matrix of your Being. What kind of environment are you emotionally labouring in? Do you feel safe and secure? Do you feel private and free from

---

and Implications for Women, Babies, and Maternity Care Childbirth Connection..

confinements? Are you feeling watched or pressured? Can you release completely and let the emotional waters wash over you or are you trying to control the outcome? Are you being supported in a loving and encouraging way?

This person acts as a trusted guide, someone who I refer to as a Midwife for the soul, who knows the terrain of both physical and spiritual labor and birth. True, you can get lost in the intensity of your soul labor as you find yourself overwhelmed, frightened, confused, frustrated, exhausted. At which point darkness can set in, causing internal unrest and mental chaos.

A powerful guide can assist in helping you find the stamina, courage, and internal power to shift these challenging states. They can hold a strong vibration of trust thus being an instrument for entrainment. This presence alone can help regulate your nervous system resulting in the capacity to *lean* in even more deeply. As you let the emotional heaviness wash through you, flood you with its intensity, it can be helpful to be grounded by the presence of such a Midwife. Although the Midwife (of the soul) cannot tell you *how* to give birth, she can offer unwavering trust in the process. She can attune to you and your breath in presence, assisting you to observe what is shifting internally. In the most expanded and enlightened way, the two of you connect to that which wants to be liberated; that which is already *alive* within. The Midwife of the soul *sees* you; *sees* into your soul; and believes in *you*.

If you relate to the term caregiver, If you work with humans in the realm of health and wholeness, if you witness transformation, if you carry the story of many, if you offer comfort and care during challenging times - then you are a 'midwife' to the space of transformation. If, however, you are *in the mess of it all* and you are searching to find your way out (through), then you are learning to be a Midwife for your Soul birth.

There is a new, yet old paradigm of thought and it is encouraging you to look closely at how you are showing up as a caregiver. For the old system is crumbling and we need to build a new way, founded in love and trust, not fear and protocol. As I come to see it, the teachings of Quantum Midwifery are Truths because they apply to all facets of life, not just birth.

Quantum Midwifery is the term coined by the Mother of The Matrona, Whapio. From my vantage point, I understand this model of care to speak to both the physical and the metaphysical elements of birth and transformation. It denotes that there is an element within birth that occurs on the quantum level – the level of energetics, subatomic, atoms, and particle and waves. The notation that to bring forth life through the portal of the physical, one needs to collapse form into particle. And, in order for this to possibly occur, form (i.e., The Mother) enters an altered state of consciousness in which any sense of self dissolves into the abyss of the *Field*. The teachings thus support how on earth a Midwife would enter such a space without disrupting the energetics of the birth-sphere.

When I heard these teachings, they penetrated deeply, and I knew they were *alive*. I practiced embodying them and sought to understand them from the depths of my soul; not just my mind. I lived them and they guided me and pulled me through my own Soul's birth. I learned how to midwife my life's labor and gathered the lessons along the way. Eventually, we morph as we evolve as part of the cellular process. There is a way through that interior door, and I am offering just another spiritual perspective.

Again, the key is always for you to find your way.

As you come close to experiencing the soul's alchemical process, it is inevitable that you will seek spiritual guidance. This quality of guidance can help you to stay anchored within your interior waters while the storm is in full force.

The Midwife of the Soul is not your anchor, nor the captain of your inner ship.

They witness, reflect, hold the tears, and encourage the process to unfold as it is, **helping you learn how to anchor in your unique soul-home.** The greatest challenge to the Midwife of the Soul is to trust in the process of transformation without needing to *save* you from the waters. Yes, she can throw out a floatation device or send out a survival boat, but she cannot row the boat for you.

To claim your Soul, you *must* engage in the interior gritty work to know that you are powerful beyond imagination. As cliché as it sounds, you can only save yourself, period. No drug. No book. No guide. No retreat. No process. No modality. Nothing can facilitate your transformation for you; your Soul is yours for claiming.

THE SACRED MIDWIFE

The room is warm, it is dark with only the light of candles flickering. There you see a shadow slowly swaying back and forth in the corner. It is the silhouette of a voluptuous pregnant gracious body, a body that is expressing her fulness and screaming to the world that it is ready to Dar La Luz (give the light).

It has been nine moons now, for which she has been the vessel that has provided this growing human nourishment, love, and safety. She has been a co-creator in this magical process and although her body has morphed during this time, it is about to morph again, as she enters this primordial time; an experience we call birth.

There is a scent to the room, a scent that denotes the ripeness. Labor is whispering the name of this, about to become, Mother. She is dancing with excitement, as she too knows that the time has come. Her unborn has incubated long enough and the discomfort of pregnancy has shifted, and has now become the butterflies of anticipation. She is filled with hope, wonder, and change; and with this change, comes great chaos. Ordered chaos, not calamity.

She sways knowing on some level that all that she once knew will forever be reorganized; a process of metamorphosis. This is the journey of birth, and the invitation to plunge into the abyss of transformation. She chooses to set sail, to release herself to the forces of labor, and to flow with the process. The unknown is terrifying, and yet, the anticipation is fueling a gentle letting go.

She leans into a willingness and efforts her attention towards the twinge of contractions, rhythmically washing over her body like waves of the ocean, she floats deeply into an altered state of consciousness. She is vigilantly aware of her external environments, and simultaneously she is immersed in her internal experience of labor. The space is quiet, with only those who love her, witnessing the unfoldment of this magnificent phenomenon. The air smells earthy, as bloody mucous secrets from her most sacred erogenous zone.

As each wave of contraction pulls her deeper into her body, the birth space carries an energetic density to it. It feels like there is a thin layer of fog, although invisible, you can feel the pressure of the air. They, her lover and Midwife, are sitting silently and in awe, as they watch the glory of her moving body. This is a woman surrendered to the pull and trusting in her body, she is empty of fear. She has already passed through the veil; the tipping point.

Her body is now deep in vortex of its primal work –
to open. It, the body, is wise and all knowing.

Birth is not foreign to her body, even though this
is her first birth. Her body is wise with DNA that
knows the portal of birth, the instinctive way of
becoming undone and morphing to give birth to
Light: Life. This is an ancient knowing and is born
from birth: Life itself. For this, she trusts in the
process of transformation and transmutation.
She has gathered all she can gather during those
nine moons. She has grown a healthy baby and
she trusts in the great wisdom of the innate
knowledge.

She hands herself over even more deeply and
her cervix continues to open, following its code.
Knowing that in order for her unborn to emerge
through her, from her, of her, she must let there
be more space. Having faith in the process, she
is ready to confront her pain. There is pain an
intensity too hard to describe with words. An
intensity that is out of the realm of ordinary, it is
altered and all-encompassing and washes over her
entire body. There are rushes crashing throughout
her system, each taking her breath away. She
collapses even further into the void.

She, for the first time, moans the sound of an
ancient voice; deep and sultry. Her moans diffuse
the pain and she regains composure. What was
that sound that just came out of her, she thinks to

herself? Barely time to ponder before she is pulled under again with the power of the oceanic force. Another moan escapes, this time louder and with more passion.

She thought she had a grip on her labor, she thought she was going to be able to handle the discomfort, she thought she was going to be able to remain conscious the entire way through - She thought she was in control.

She is confronted by another wave that engulfs her entirely, flailing for air, she forgets to moan this time. She was mistaken, she is no longer in control of this journey; something greater and more powerful is. She rests her brow between the rushes and lays her head down on the side of her lover, as she sleeps for a thousand years in between contractions.

Pulled out of this dreamless state, she breathes deeply as her eyes roll back into her head, and this time, she lets out a guttural roar. It feels to her that it is lasting a lifetime. She wants to fight against the sensations, as they are so foreign to her, but her roar carries her through. This time, she manages to keep her head above water. She has found her rhythm. To her lover, it all seems to appear so graceful. He sits in silence, in meditative wonder, and holds her head between contractions. Lightly brushing her check with kisses of tender loving care.

In the opposite corner, of this very sacred space, rocks the gentle presence of a wise woman. She too sways, but to her own rhythm. She has a confidence about her; a strength and wisdom that runs deep. She knows the intimacy of birth, she trusts in birth, and she bears witness to the Mystery. All is calm in her internal world, fully present. Her silent strength is an indication that all is as should be. She smiles, as she notices the Lover's soothing touch.

This beauty of a figure, this caregiver, this Midwife knows the sensuality and sexuality of labor and birth. She knows her place and she bows in honor every time she is invited into a sanctuary of birth. This is not a process to disturb, but rather, witness with absolute presence. She is a grounding force, a rock, and roots the laboring woman with her wisdom.

As the mother struggles to find her way, each time she falls deeper into her labor and is ready to endure the increasingly more intense wave of contractions. The room is shifting, and the woman is challenged to find her comfort again. So foreign are these deep sensations, so wide has she opened, so loud has she moaned. The waves are crashing in on top of one another, she senses she is being pulled. And she opens her eyes (for the first time in a long time) and reaches for help. "Too much to bear alone," she hollers.

"I can't do this anymore," she cries.
"Take it all away, I am done, so done," she wails.
"Do it for me, take my baby out of me," she weeps.
"I am about to die," she collapses.

And in this collapse, the wise one walks over to her, lovingly holds her head in the palm of her hands and looks her deep into the eyes. She speaks to her soul and she says with a smile, "You have come so far, you have endured so much, you are almost done, and you and only you, can find the inner power to birth your baby." With her serious, yet gentle voice, she continues, "And you will find this fierce power, you must go deeper yet, you must let it all go, you must drop fully into this Mystery, only you *know* how to do this."

The mother is left to weep in a moment of despair, sure, that she is dying, sure that she cannot go any further. Nothing is smooth about this moment, the beauty has shifted from an ethereal quiet and calmness to a frantic, primal, animalistic environment. And with that, something so raw and powerful floods her body. A force like nothing ever before experienced, and it rushes through her entire system and moves her baby down through her birth canal. With this ecstatic rush of fire, this Woman lets out a sound that could shatter the earth, and she stands back and witnesses herself crown her baby. She knows, she did not move her baby through the birth canal with will alone, it was this Force: Life itself, that shot through her like lightening. Every cell in her body knew what the message of that force was, and they all morphed to create more space, to let her baby through.

Crowning, about to be born, she places her hands on the head of the baby. And with the next rush of power, she releases the head. The power in her hands will forever be remembered as she brought her baby's head into the world. Suspended between both worlds now. Only a power out of this world could cause a force that big. And now she waits as she looks into the eyes of her lover and her Midwife. They all nod in anticipation of the next washing of a contraction. And this Mother is eagerly waiting, with a ravenous energy about her, ready to birth her baby into her own hands.

She kneels, with one knee up, supported by her lover and she *knows*, like no other knowing, that she has found her power as she brings forth new life. Here she rests for a moment, orienting herself, and looking into the eyes of this wide-open new Being. She pauses, wipes her tears, and lifts her child to her chest. The room is hot, so hot that everyone is sweating. The baby barely cries as she gasps at her first breath. The energy is calm, thick, and powerful. There is a smell in the room, a smell of earth and blood. Mixed together with the essence of love; the smell of birth. There is no rush, no bright lights, no loud noises. All those present are calm as everyone soaks up the aroma of bliss.

Her lover wipes her brow and kisses her lips. Together they melt into one as oxytocin floods the bodies of many. She, the Midwife, walks over and kisses her forehead. Tenderly she touches her abdomen. There is blood, and this is comforting and normal. The new Mother opens her eyes, glistening with joy, and speaks, "Thank you, I did it." A tear falls, a tear of appreciation and honor. And the Midwife responds, "And I knew you would." The room is reassuring, the energy shifting, as the Mother moves to her bed. Standing up, she has one final contraction, and births the placenta. The Midwife holds the placenta in her hands, looks into it as if it carried magic, and nods in affirmation. All is well. She wraps the placenta in cloth and lays it next to the nursing newborn.

The sacred space, dark and full of hope, is quietly being cleaned: cleansed. The new family is cradled in their bed, with their nakedness keeping everyone warm. And the Midwife, sings songs of welcoming and birth, as she brews hot teas and nourishes this new family. As time fades, she the Mother, is exhausted from all the work. The lover is exhausted from holding her space; and the Midwife is ready to lay her head down. And so, she packs her bags, bids a loving farewell to this lovely couple, and shuts the door oh so quietly. And so, it lasts forever.

As the Great Mother: The Midwife, returns to her home, she remembers the Tao of Midwifery:

The midwife completes her work by doing nothing,
She teaches without speaking a word.
Things arise, and she lets them come;
Things leave, and she lets them go.
Creating, not possessing;
facilitating, yet laying no claim.
And when her work is done, she forgets about it.
And so, it lasts forever.

She bows her head in humility offering a prayer of gratitude, for she has been graced and honored to witness the power of transformation yet again. She carries these stories dear to her heart and knows the Magic in their wisdom. She herself, has gone through the fire of transformation and *knows* the Force that takes over. For as she has been the midwife and witness to hundreds of births, she too, had to learn how to midwife her own birth: Soul's birth.

Journal Entry

Your work is *Holy* work. You are not doing the
healing; the Divine is. The Great Spirit is Creation.
Let it be. Let it in. Bow. Kneel. The mind wants to
know, the mind wants to return to the ordinary.
But everything is extraordinary. I will be held.
Protect yourself, it is not your job to do their work.
Your work is done. When the fairy tale is alive
and told, when past meets up with present time, a
portal opens. His death opened up a portal – past,
present, future is one. Just listen. LISTEN. What
happens when the fairy tale collides with present
time? When the fairy tale is not separate, but in
moment motion?

THE HOLISTIC STAGES OF *Labour*

She travels to the edge of her reality, of herself, **parts the Veil and goes beyond**. *The Veil is that curtain that separates ordinary reality from the Altered State...Mothers may approach the Veil several times before deciding to move through. Circumstances may also prevent the mother from moving through. Constant questioning, especially about mundane affairs, and interruptions in mother's rhythm serve to bring mother back to ordinary reality. At this point the mother becomes more silent and others in attendance naturally do the same. ~ Whapio*

EMBARKATION

*Embarkation is also the time when a woman realizes that labor is truly here. Mother is excited, maybe a bit nervous, concerned for the welfare of her loved ones having made sure that they will be well taken care of while **she is gone.**
-Whapio*

THE GREAT CATALYST

Anthony Robbins, in his works called The Edge, expresses that we need the discomfort; we need to be disturbed and feel the pain in order to grow and change. When we are disturbed long enough something within us stirs, awakens, and screams ENOUGH. In this instance, your labor has begun, and you are now **embarking upon a journey of awakening** (if you so choose).

I know I am repeating myself here as I continue to prove a point, an important one to keep coming back to. The point being that life's wounds can be purposeful. There comes a time in your life when you experience a life circumstance so powerful that it causes intense turbulence and an emotional inner collapse. The kind of emotional (and spiritual) collapse that I am referring to is known as grief, despair, anguish, shame and rage.

Maybe you are in it right now, or are coming out of it?

It can feel like your life is disjointed, unfair, overwhelming, and unjust. The heaviness of the experience often comes to you as a surprise, completely out of your ordinary reality. The coping strategies that you once used are no longer working to keep this 'force' at bay - The force of change, the force of chaos, the force of distress, the force of your very own emotional soul labor.

When you are grief stricken due to the gravity of your personal circumstances, you become shocked into the present moment, as the intensity of this emotional weight is too much to ignore. For some, you may not have experienced the emotional heaviness as of yet, because you are managing to keep this energy of transformation far away; not quite ready to *lean* into the experience. The personal circumstance that has caused you to pause, and begin the process of decent, becomes the catalyst for huge transformation. Not all initiations begin with trauma. Some choose to be initiated through spiritual rituals. Others are initiated through the door of ecstasy and soul sex. In ancient times, initiation was part of growing up and becoming an adult. These induced forms of initiation are somewhat controlled, in that they are managed through ritual and preparation. In a way childbirth is a controlled initiation. However, even in preparation for such transformative events, there is always an element of losing control.

Trauma however, our soul wounds, act as an initiator. However, it often comes as a surprise in that we have not had the opportunity to prepare mentally and spiritually for such a quest.

Which is why it is so fucken hard to grapple with.

A catalyst is something that enters your life, stirs up necessary chaos, and then removes itself from your life. It never remains as a constant or permanent occurrence, but rather temporary, until the necessary changes have been set in action. It is upon you to find the courage to engage this catalyst with full attention and awareness – to see it for what it is, a catalyst.

Although incredibly powerful, and often painful, the experience itself (the reason for the collapse) becomes your greatest allay in assisting you towards deeper awareness of yourself, and in return, healing and transformation. Without a catalyst, humans will instinctively resist their darker emotions; the catalyst acts as a necessary evil.

Collectively, we are imprinted to keep the lurking heavy feelings hidden. The catalyst provides an opportunity to explore and investigate what lives deep within, below the surface of ordinary reality. Change and transformation cannot occur without a union of your entire Being; this I call wholeness and integration.

When you keep those hidden and challenging emotions away from your heart, you will never truly know wholeness. The heart heals and transforms the pain of the chaos into healing

energy and in return blows open all those areas
that remain grid locked. If healing is indeed what
you seek (for the soul is always seeking wholeness
& integration) then experiencing the collapse is
a key process. Within the collapse, you venture
into the land of a soulful labor and birth process,
as the power of grief moves through you like
contractions to assist in your inner awakening.

What catalyst(s) are you facing in your life?

EMBARKATION

Your **embarkation begins when you feel this pull of your life's labor**. You hear the call of a distant voice. There is internal discord, an irritation, and you choose to pay attention in ways that you have not yet. There is a rhythm, a beat, a pulse carrying you in the distance. This is the beginning of the surrender.

With a woman in labor, she feels the faint pull of her early contractions. She knows labor is about to begin and she is getting ready to go on this journey. She has no knowing as of yet, how this labor will play out. She knows not the intensity she is about to face, but she is pulled to *lean in*, regardless. For some this is a time of great excitement and anticipation. For others it is riddled with fear. It is the beginning of great change, for birth equals change.

During this time, the call and pull gets louder and louder; and the rhythm of contractions increase in speed and intensity. Soon the woman will no longer be able to stay conscious in her everyday reality; soon the internal pull will take her under. There comes a need to tune out the exterior world and tune into her interior.

The ego silences as the power of the unknown moves to the forefront. The intensity of the contractions tunes out the ego mind. A new kind of trust embodies a Woman in labor, if encouraged and allowed. For to fight this stage, one will remain 2 cm – 3 cm dilated for many hours or days. Eventually, hopefully, exhaustion will take over and the woman is called to surrender to the flow.

This phase of the journey introduces a very important notion: To pay less attention to the external world, and tune into the interior landscape. In doing so, the mother lets go of taking care of life's external demands. **The contractions invite her to go within and *listen*.** She cannot take her comforts with her; she cannot take her loved ones. Embarking requires that you/she/ the Mother agree to be initiated. Although it may appear that the Mother does not have any choice in what is about to unfold, in fact she does. It is an act of inner will to say yes to process of birth.

In your life, this call is often quiet at first. It may feel like an internal irritant, something you know you need to face but have been ignoring for some time now. This irritant gets louder until you have no other choice but to pay attention. For some, you are thrown into your embarkation with no preparation at all; a death, a loss of some sort, a traumatic event can cause labor to begin without any warning. Suddenly grief is at your soul's doorstep, pain is lurking, and you are not ready to open it. And yet, choice is still necessary to move deeper into the process that is unfolding.

Take time to pause on this phase of your journey. What did your embarkation look and feel like? Are you still embarking, afraid to spiral deeper into the abyss of your soul's labor? Are you still gestating; 8 or 9 months pregnant but feel the pull? What are you most afraid of? Can you feel something nudging internally? Have you been swept away into the waterfall of grief?

Journal Entry

"What we cannot hold, we cannot process. What we cannot process, we cannot transform. What we cannot transform, haunts us...When we bury feelings, we bury them alive" – Ron Siegel.

Integration is health - Memories and emotions are no longer split off. Heart and head connected; mind and body connected. We are okay with who we are; why we are; how we are. We split off because feelings were too hard to bear; too difficult to integrate. Notice what it is. Recognize what's happening. Allow experience to be what it is. Investigate inner experiences with kindness and non-identification. It is not personal; impersonal. Always, it has been that way.

ENTERING THE VEIL

The Mother reaches a point in her traveling where it is time for her to go alone. The endorphins released by her body during her embarking have begun to change her consciousness and she enters, more deeply, the realm of the altered state. She travels to the edge of her normal reality, parts the Veil and goes beyond. **The Veil is my nomenclature for the curtain that separates ordinary reality from the deep altered state.** *~Whapio*

Straddling Two Worlds

In the beginning, after we have indeed embarked and the initiation is in flow, we are straddling two worlds: the exterior rational world and the interior soul world. As stated over and over again, birth happens instinctively from the non-rational plane of existence. We must enter the Mystery and altered states of reality to let the magic of birth occur. What does all this really mean?

Humans crave the altered state; we are naturally seeking to be in contact with the Mystery, the Divine, or Source Energy – the essence of who we are. Life itself. Both the metaphysical and neuroscience perspectives indicate that all healing, all spiritual and mystical experiences, all peak performances, all ecstatic states, and all journeys of transformation occur when in altered brainwave states. Extensive research indicates that there are five measurable brainwave patterns, and these are Beta, Alpha, Theta, Delta, and Gamma.[14]

---

[14] Dispenza, J. (2017). **Becoming Supernatural**. California: Hay House Inc.

Beta: This is normal waking reality. Most of the world functions in beta reality. We communicate in beta, we work in beta, we even think in beta. Beta dominates our world. But if we never dropped out of beta states, we would die, for we cannot function optimally only in Beta. We need beta reality; considered the most advanced brainwave frequency. High beta indicates survival and stress response. Long term high beta state is connected to illness and deterioration of health. Our system is not meant to operate in high beta, long term. However, given the nature of our current environment, high beta is the norm for many. Resulting in high amounts of stress chemicals being dumped into our system and activating constricted emotions of fear and anger. It is important to note that high amounts of stress chemicals are contraindicative to instinctive birth.[15]

Alpha: This brain wave state is the daydreaming state, the place of visualization. When we close our eyes and take in a couple deep breaths, we drop into Alpha. For some, you can experience a flood of comfort and relaxation within your body. We can see vivid imagery while in Alpha and can easily access this state during waking times –

---

[15] Buckley, S. (2015). *Hormonal Physiology of Childbearing: Evidence and Implications for Women, Babies, and Maternity Care.* Childbirth Connection.

All we need to do is close our eyes and breathe deeply. Anytime we focus our attention internally, consciously breathe, we drop into Alpha. Alpha is the state of walking and waking meditation. For some, they spend most of their time in this state. Alpha is involved with the creative self. In some circles it is considered to be the bridge between ordinary and non-ordinary reality. It is the *wave* that shifts our attention towards deeper states of being. It would be curious to assess a Mother's brain wave patterns during labour. My guess is that the Mother shifts into Alpha brain wave frequency during her period of embarkation.

Theta: Dropping deeper and slower in brainwave frequency and into the self, with eyes closed in silence and stillness, we can feel the soothing presence of theta. In theta, small self dissolves and Soul self emerges. The ego is no longer at the forefront and we can experience an expanded sense of Self. It has been noted that healing happens in theta states. We naturally slow down when we are not well and there is a need for the stillness of theta. The body is so intelligent and knows how to heal; it knows how to give birth, all without the need of external help – Brilliant!

Theta healing techniques are about stimulating this state within using sound patterns, and then reprogramming belief systems so that deep healing can occur. When we enter deep,still mediation, where the mind silences and we drift off into 'never land' we are tapping into theta states. Great insight can occur in Theta. It is believed that most inventors and healers drop into theta often and gather information beyond the ego. Theta is the state of the healer within.

Delta: Here in lays your soul, your depths, your abyss, your deep blue. There is silence, stillness, nothingness, yet total knowing and connection with all that is. Those who speak of delta states indicate that language cannot explain, for when in delta, one is no longer an individual self.
Deep dreamless states of sleep bring us in touch with Delta. This brainwave state is slow and deep; profound.

Gamma: The state of ecstasy. It is noted that humans who experience gamma flow states, recount feeling in union with the Divine. Gamma is associated with peak experiences and flow states. When measured and charted it can be interpreted as if the person is having a seizure. Gamma is the Mother Juice; the *Light*.

When we enter the veil, we step out of our normal ego reality of existence and we allow ourselves to enter a deeper internal state of the unknown. We go into our soul and we lose contact and care with the external world. All that matters is the labor and navigating it with awareness and presence. Psychedelics are often used as a catalyst to move beyond the veil; to drop the ego. The ego does not want to lose touch with reality, it will do everything in its power to maintain control. Inducing altered states helps to disempower the ego. And, labor does just that, if allowed to.

During labor, when the mother has entered the veil, this is a time when the air in the room takes on a different density. Yes, although this cannot be measured, it is something that is felt. There is a weight and a sacred silence in the energy of the space that happens when the labor progresses to this stage. If we were to measure the physical dilation and progression of labor, a woman would be around 5-8 cm. The tides of contractions are stronger and closer together and the mother is finding her internal flow; and now she deepens and softens her surrender. Time stops or rather takes on a different form. The sense is that of timelessness; absolute presence.

In life's labor, you might experience this as a need to pay attention to that which is causing you discomfort. The pain and intensity of the process has become louder and present, and you can no longer ignore the pull or the pain. The call for surrender is no longer a whisper, but a need. You choose to step deeper into your soul's labor and let the emotional debris sweep through your system and heart. You are allowing the process, choosing to no longer fight it.

If you ignore this stage, you will exhaust yourself
trying to control it and keep this calling at bay.
You know you are called to grow, expand, undo
and move beyond that which keeps you stuck. You
cannot, with force, hold up the internal dam. You
are being asked to go deeper. Will you listen to this
call?

I knew I had entered the veil as I was catapulted
into a state of deep grief. Everything about this
experience felt so familiar. The waves of grief,
stemming from somewhere deeper than my
gut, rushed through me in a familiar rhythm. As
I moaned, I felt timeless. I no longer identified
with Jennifer, for I knew not what I was or what
was happening. All I did know for certain was that
something was happening, and it was outside of my
control. And so, I surrendered.

In anguish, I fought and flailed at times. I hated
what was happening and wanted to destroy myself
in the process. On my knees, as I wept, I pleaded
for it all to stop. I begged for a reason why; the
rational mind, always wanting to hook itself and
find meaning.

Nothing made sense anymore, that which I had
built my life upon was in question. I thought
this was one big cosmic joke and I had already
suffered enough. I did not surrender peacefully
or gracefully; I will tell you that. Eventually
though, after being stripped raw (like the descent

of Inanna) I finally let *go*. It was then, after the encounter with humility, that I felt the presence of grace; the Angel of grace. In that moment, I *knew* I was in labor.

BETWEEN THE WORLDS:
Riding the Waves

During this time the Mother craves privacy, silence, warmth and the intimacy of the dark. She looks to her Guardian to know that she is safe and that no one will breach the sacredness of her travels by distracting her or leveling any expectations on her. - Whapio

Riding the Waves

Once you have entered the veil and the labor is real (not induced or contrived) all you can do is ride it through. Learning how to follow your labor is part of the learning process. Trust me; it is not neat and clean. It is messy, raw and real, expressive and at times, volatile. Then, when you finally surrender in presence, there is peace and grace that cleanses your soul.

I laugh at myself now, why did I fight it so much? I knew that it is the resistance to the flow that causes so much more pain and chaos. Yet I believe that this struggle is a necessary part of the journey towards wholeness and ego death. Therefore, I say, fight away, flail, roar, scream, cry, anguish, rage, and get the energy out – this way you will go deeper.

You have surrendered and the journey has begun. Your soul labor is active within and you are experiencing the waves of contractions. Life's labor pains are pulsing through you, coursing through the marrow of your being. *You are in it and really, **there is no going back***. The pull to birth is moving you forward, and yet, there is no easy way through. All you can do is ride each wave with as much consciousness, embodiment, and presence as possible.

Pay attention to the contractions and do not run from the pain. This is a necessary and critical phase of labor. If you choose to numb yourself, detach from the intensity of the labor, fight against the flow of emotion, or escape by way of drugs; you will miss the opportunity to find, in consciousness, your internal power to give birth to that which is wanting to be born.

Although riding the waves can be exhausting, overwhelming, frightening, painful, intense, and all encompassing, it is the only way through to the other side. It is incumbent upon you to *feel, not think,* your way through it and express yourself as needed. You are invited to meet your internal pain full on, move through the pain, and in return find relief, all the while, allowing your birth to be soul-directed.

The deeper you go into the experience, the more you will learn, gather and carry with you. This is the ultimate practice in surrendering and trusting that there is purpose in the pain.

Remember that with each rush of energy, burst of overwhelming grief or despair, you are moving closer towards a state of internal peace.

When we are encouraged, feel safe, and trust this journey, we are able to flow with life's labor pains and progression occurs. Most do not want to be alone during this time, for it can be intensely overwhelming and yet, you must be with the sensations on your own. There is a difference between being *left alone* versus needing to *be alone*. This is a journey of internal navigation and birthing.

There is something powerful about being witnessed versus watched; held in trust and encouragement versus being told what to do; loved and nurtured versus someone taking charge of your situation. The presence of a Midwife (a guiding force), one who works in this paradigm of thought, can bring much comfort to this journey. Just knowing that someone believes in you, trusts in this process of labor, and encourages you to keep dropping into the labor, can bring much added strength.

During this spiral of labor, you are becoming undone.

Each contraction is building on the other, and the intensity increases as your labor progresses. You are in the soup, the cosmic soup, the juice of metamorphosis. You have become no-thing; yet your consciousness is aware of everything. Form is disappearing into particle. You are creating space; space to bring forth life.

Seriously, take this in for a minute. When a mother is between worlds, she is in an expanded state of consciousness. She is wild, vulnerable, instinctive, creature like, and completely untethered. If she has collapsed in trust to Life itself, she has handed her ego over to the Great- Not-There. And, the energy of birth has taken over to guide the way. Why would anyone want to intervene here? Disrupt the flow? Take charge? Manage? Control? Why would we *ever* want to get in the way of this moment of divine union? It is insanity, actually. And, it stems from fear. We want to control that which is uncontrollable; Life itself, cannot be controlled. But our ego will do everything in its power to try to maintain any veneer of control.

I will reiterate: the *work* is to lean into trusting Life itself with all your being and body. Practicing in this quality of trust builds soul stamina. At this juncture, you are encountering the next edge. Do not give up now and be swallowed by despair, darkness, and death. This is your fight for life and light. You are nearing the end: You are returning home to your soul.

THE ART OF SURRENDER

During the decent, a force much greater than your ego self pulls you towards the earth, and there you are on your knees with your head hung low. You never imagined that you would find yourself relinquishing power and handing it over to 'something' much stronger and more powerful than you alone. Still unsure whether or not you fully trust in this invisible force, you find yourself lost and exhausted without anything to anchor *you* in. And, you no longer recognize this *you* that needs to be anchored.

An anchor grounds you, holding your centre during times of great storm; It holds you close, helping you to trust the process. What is your anchor? What can you hold on to? This phase of surrendering arrives during a critical time when you feel fragile and weakened by the emotional collapse. You have been riding the waves for some time now; between the worlds. You may feel like you can no longer resist a Universal power that has been whispering your name.

Eventually, stamina runs out and you acknowledge that you alone, cannot endure the intensity of the internal mayhem. This is a turning point along the healing path in which humility is experienced in an authentically derived way. Your ego recognizes that it no longer has power over your internal and external circumstances. For some, humility comes in prayer and acknowledgement of your current state. For others, it is experienced when you recognize that all that you thought you knew and were, is no longer true. When you surrender to this state, you release the need to energetically fight 'what is' and rather, you choose to look reality straight in the eye.

It is here, in these moments of silence and surrender, where you commune with the Mystery (that which is beyond rational reality) and you begin to initiate conversation with this 'part' of the soul-self. Some experience this as prayer; for others it is communion or deep contemplation. The point to consider is that you begin to notice and sense that you are no longer alone on this path; and you never were. You are being guided and held in love. Bathed in the glory of this profound love. Your heart is activated and for some (like me), for the very first time.

Through surrendering you begin to experience the different textures of these altered states. In my experience, it took a lot to 'bring me to my knees' so to speak. This was not a graceful process, however, when I finally lowered my head and silenced my mind, a shift occurred in which I was *shown* a way. Had I never reached this phase of grief and healing; I would not have been able to hear what my deepest, most intimate part of my soul was saying to me. From here I was able to let the pain of grief wash over and through me, like a contraction in labor, carrying me forward towards a new state of Being. It was during this moment that I clung to the holistic stages of labor as my guiding metaphor. They unfolded, in my third eye, as Truths to be tested.

I knew that the voices of destruction would pull me out from behind the veil, disrupting the flow of connection and rhythm. By becoming intimate with these inner voices, I began to unravel from that which prevented me from knowing my true nature. The dance between reality (as I knew it) and non-ordinary reality is ever present. One moment you have given yourself over to the flow of grief, present and empty. In another moment, you are shocked out of that state by those destructive inner voices. The small self wants to remain in control; at front and centre. The push and pull, back and forth, nature of this soul tango *is* the work of labor.

By discovering the inner tools to disarm the power of negative mental chatter, you begin to breathe life into those dormant parts of the self. You begin to feel what it is like to have true power within and you know you have the courage and stamina to take hold of your life.

Perhaps for the first time, you receive a glimpse of what it might feel like to be *alive*. At this point, there is an opening. You are on the verge of summoning this power; the great gate of transition.

THE SUMMONING: *Transition*

Mother becomes aware that she is nearing the peak. She is deep in a vortex, past anything she has ever known.. **She has been continuously opening to wisdom, opening to revelation and now she comes face to face with the apex of her labor**. This is what she has come for – accessing the new spirit, the new person that is her child and her Partner's child, and bringing this soul to Earth. She hears the Summons, she summons her child and together they make their way bac. - Whapio.

HITTING THE EDGE OF CHANGE

Ah yes, the moment in labor where all women have had enough. We scream out in pain, we are so undone, so wide open, so intensely manipulated on the inside in ways unimaginable. How can we go on, how can this continue without a death; without dying? During the transitional time, a woman in labor usually has a final giving up, a plea with all those present to remove the discomfort, take it away and finish the journey for her.

It is normal to want to assist a woman during this time. To witness this kind of desperation and to do *nothing* can be very challenging for those watching from the corners. Yet one knows (if she really knows) that the time is near for the birth when she reaches the moment of bargaining. The pain is peaking in intensity and about to change, and labor is taking on a different tone. The energy in the room is activated. The scent of birth is evident.

At this point in labour, the Mother is encouraged to perform an *act of will* and summon every last bit of strength and stamina that she never knew existed within. She is almost done – so she is often told. The hard work of opening and surrendering over and over again is nearing its end. The chaos has reached its peak, and all one must do is finally *die to that which they once knew.*

Let these final contractions transform you, roar, and allow your labor to be heard. Find your creature, your animal voice, and bear down to the final openings. That which you once knew is no longer; it is time to say good-bye and open to the portal of potential to that which will be born. This is a point of conscious choice.

Transition is a glorious chaotic time.

Some have found humor during this time, have had peak experiences of orgasmic chaos. The intensity is wonderful if embraced. Most encouraging is that you can promise yourself that you are almost done. So, pull up your socks, draw upon your internal strength and find that determination to keep on going.

I will tell you this: the kind of power I am speaking about cannot come from your ego-self. This is a Force within that is cosmic; one that can move mountains and is awe-inducing. Nothing is normal during this time, except that you become that which is no longer normal. The only thing normal, is that everything changes, and you scream out against all that has bound you – you are becoming unbound and on the cusp of major change. Keep going, keep going, and keep going; you have come this far, you are nearing the end.

Emptying to Become No-thing

Eventually your ego completely dissolves during the process of soul-birthing. You have been faced with the arduous task of surrendering to the pull of your emotional and spiritual labor. You endured grief and despair and rage. You let the powerful emotions rush through you, without letting them become you. Twisting your inner soul so tightly that you wanted to vomit afterwards. You have challenged or been challenged by your beliefs and ideologies and have learned the art of internal investigation. You found the courage to face your 'enemies' and discovered resolution and understanding. You have taught yourself new skills to communicate your needs and are able to identify patterns in your life that are destructive, both mentally and externally. You've experienced humility and have felt lost and alone.

The entire egoic structure that you have identified with for so long is no longer true.

You *know* that you are not 'that person' anymore, and you *never* were. It was all a façade that your ego has nicely orchestrated so you could survive in this world. Now is the opportunity you have been waiting for, to re- claim your authentic self (isn't this what all the new age spiritual books speak about and we all want)? What they have failed to tell us is how hard we have to work to claim our soul. Trust me, your ego is going to fight you, she wants to maintain power and control over your life. She likes her identity and feels very safe as 'Ms. So and So'.

In order for you to shed your skin, you must shed your identity as well.

Simply knowing that this is part of the process can decrease any internal resistance to this experience. As humans we tend to take ourselves too seriously (I am as serious as a heart- attack), and in so doing, we lose out on life. We are too caught up in protecting our self-image that we forget to engage with Life itself, in all its glory.

Your summoning brings you close to *knowing* your soul and claiming your authentic voice, which starts to become louder than your ego voice. This voice knows the way, although it may be hard to hear initially, it does become louder over time. Not in the overt loud ways, like screaming, but rather, our *knowing* becomes louder because we are learning how to deeply listen. In the experience of 'nothingness' you are filled with pure potential and a life force so great, that your life's meaning becomes illuminated. From this state, your internal power fills you with new motivation; no longer needing to escape the discomfort but rather, encouraged to go over the edge.

To fly.

At this point on the path, I understood it to be the moment when I experienced great understanding. I saw with clear inner eyes my entire life in review – forwards and backwards. The victim stories I held, that kept parts of me in the dungeon, could no longer hold together. They were changing. I held my inner parts with tremendous compassion and released their pain. My life had meaning, not intellectual meaning, but rather *myth meaning*. I was wide open and receptive to Life's 10 cm mark.

THE *Quietude*: THE RESTING PHASE

"This is **the period of great stillness and peace that occurs after transition**. All becomes calm and quiet and the Mother knows that IT has happened. She knows she has found what she is looking for...her still place in the tempest and access to the soul of her baby. - Whapio

THE QUIESCENCE

In this newfound humility and lack of ego identity there is space to breathe now, and a release of bound up energy floods the matrix of your Being. You have dissolved and are standing on the edge of change. You can still feel some resistance and tension within as you continue to follow your breath and are reminded that you are indeed still *alive*.

Thus far, you have energetically and soulfully worked incredibly hard. During this phase you are asked to rest and recuperate. As a mother endures the work of labor, she too, needs to find solace in the arms of her loved ones (whether that be her partner, care giver, or Divine Source); she allows herself to be embraced, nurtured, and deeply held as she is replenished with life force.

In this quiescence, a necessary pause, you experience an internal reorganization. You may, for the first time, be experiencing contact with your Soul; a force so fluid, powerful, animated, deep, profound, and inspired. Here in lies the essence of your authenticity, power, and purpose. It is from here, that you are carried forward by the presence of Grace; literally infused with energy that comes from a power outside of your conscious reality.

Birth, when untouched, is magical. I say this because although our womanly bodies are created to give birth, it is magic that expands and contorts our physiology in such a manner to allow the passage to open and release a baby.

I saw, during my own births, my cells expand to create space within – total utter space – and I saw that we are indeed created by particles colliding together and always creating space.

It is within the space, the pause of chaos, which allows for the regeneration and re-integration of the self to reformulate. Space is how and where the magic occurs. During this pivotal time of rest, while on the precipice of transformation, you gather your strength to give birth to yourself anew.

You begin to be filled with inner power and a desire to move forth with passion and purpose. Patterns of pain, destruction, and calamity fall away, and life takes on a new texture and meaning. The being you once were, is no longer a dominate figure, and a new soul infused Being awakens. This takes conscious effort, for the privilege lies in the power of choice. It is here, saturated with an inner power and a determination to make different choices, that you align yourself with all the power of the Universe and know that you are indeed one.

Our bodies are magnificent, and our soul is glorious. After experiencing the peak chaos of your labor, do you think you would be thrown into the work of giving birth? The answer is no, you are given a period of grace, a time of peace, silence, and calm – a quiescence. During this time, just breathe. Think of nothing and notice the space that exists within. There was a clearing, and now there is calmness. You are encouraged to listen to the voice within, your soul's yearning.

Whapio said that during this time, "[You] will **receive wisdom** that is easily accessible at this great altitude and in this momentous altered state." Gather this information and tuck it away, remembering what she spoke of. This is your encounter with grace, and you have been given a glimpse of that which is about to be born; that which is waking up from the curse. The curse of trauma-land. Fall in love with this insight. Listen deeply to your soul's yearning.

This may be your first meeting with your Soul voice; hear her sing. Weep in silence as you listen, *really* listen. You have gone through a huge gate and you endured the contractions of despair; experience this peace-fullness. Be bathed by your soul. All the while know that your work is not finished. If only we could hang out here forever. You are reorganizing on a cellular level, rebuilding resources so you can break free from your cocoon and spread those wings.

No-Body

The day I stopped needing
To be a somebody
Quiet
Blanketed the tightly bound
Somebody
Warmth
Unfurled its petals
As it drank from this nourishment
For the very
First
Time.
You can rest now
Said the voice from the well.
You, *can* rest now
Said *that* voice from the well.
Laying down its sword
After the long
Long battle
It could never win
Enslaved by exhaustion
Dissolving
Into no-body
Rest
Rest
Rest
Said the voices from the wells.

THE BREAKERS –
The Birthing Tides

Usually mothers seem to be at one with the power of the waves and push with them but I have witnessed a few women who never actively push during their labors. The uterus does everything. Mothers articulate with these birthing contractions and the birthing song that began in early labor crescendos into magnificent aria. **The mother's voice may actually guide the baby to the end of the tunnel**. *These universal sounds may spur the baby on through his or her journey and create the natural excitement and tension that comes with reaching a goal. - Whapio*

You are wide open to life and ready to claim your soul; this is the finale. If only it were that easy, to be able to get this far and somehow be handed your unborn baby without further work. Yet, **you are required to give birth**. You have done the work of facing the intensity of your labor and it is true, the pain has now shifted. With effort and vitality, you use this newfound power within to give birth. I have seen mothers lose stamina at this stage. The defeat in their eyes can be horrifying. They are instructed to push, often against instincts. Often there is a desire to rush this process. I liken this to pushing against the stream.

By this point, metaphorically speaking, you are now in union with your soul. You have encountered Truth within, and you are working with Her, no longer alone. Ready to give birth, to new Life. Your purpose in the chaos is clear, and your determination is strong. The quest is to animate your soul, so it comes to forefront of your life to lead. No longer in hiding or dormancy, *she* is about to be known.

Although tempting, do not abort this process, for it is when the cusp of transformation. In a physical birth, the baby is traveling through the region of the birth canal; yet the unborn is traversing worlds. During this phase of the labor, I experienced only space. My babies wanted to be born and they were demanding that I be stretched open in ways so foreign to my physical body. It was the image of space, noticing that nothing is solid, and everything is malleable, that calmed this intensity.

When the birthing tides take over, *nothing* can stop the rush of life force. The power of pushing, when instinctive, is infused with the energy of life itself. Life *wants* to be born!

Only a power unknown to the ego can give birth and contort the body in such a way. To not believe in the mystical at this pivotal point is mere ignorance. For the combination of will and the quantum field are involved in this final push-through. When this new soul-force flows through you, one can only get out of the way, because the creative life force of birth is the most powerful unifying force.

To reiterate: it is not the will of the mother alone that gives birth to the new life. It is the will of *new Life itself*; this combined with the internal power of the mother. Your Soul desires to be birthed anew. Having been silenced for so long it has a yearning of its own to make it through the canal. Your Soul's desire combined with your will to live is the recipe to make it through this final spiral of labor. Feel this internal stamina and let that which wants to thrive, come *alive*.

THE EMERGENCE: *Birth*

At the time of Crowning the largest part of the baby's head has now passed through the Birth Gate. Mother is often ecstatic and totally energized. She may cry out as if to announce her return.- Whapio

Awakening as you Push

Embodying this new state of empowerment is indeed magnificent and a feat to be proud of. From this stage of awareness, you notice that everything was perfectly aligned; all the chaos, the pain, the challenges, the drama - your entire life thus far has been perfectly orchestrated. Granted, this does not diminish any horrible acts you have had to endure and overcome; it means you are no longer governed or haunted by the memories.

Relief overwhelms you. While in the center of the chaos, you may not have been able to notice this constant forward motion, with purpose. However, now standing back from the storm and on the other side of transformation, you can see (with an awakened interior eye) how nothing ever remains the same (nor is it ever supposed to).

From these perspectives, there is no room for regret or blame (with remorse having been experienced earlier along the path as you came to know forgiveness). True understanding is upon you and you are filled with authentic gratitude that is born from this deep well within. You have gathered information that awakens you to 'see' the wisdom in all of your soul's wounds. It is from this lens that you can now re-write your story, your life's story with new meaning and depth. This 'story' contains wisdom, polished and excavated by you, and it is the wisdom (born out of the wound) that you will share with the world.

No longer is this tale told from the standpoint of the wounded victim but rather the victoriously healed. The power, strength, courage, stamina and trust that have been built during this time of deep soul transformation will never leave you, and therefore, forever guide you. From here on forth, you carry this inner wisdom that you discovered by finding your way through the painful mayhem. As you exhale, you allow for a great pause, noticing everything with joy filled tears.

Inhalation integrates this knowledge into your cellular makeup; the marrow of your being.

Once your soul has become animated and merged with the rest of your Being, it can no longer lay sleeping, dormant. I have been told that it is incumbent from here on forth to use this power wisely and let your ignited soul lead, making choices that are aligned with a powerful source of Universal energy, to create goodness and spread love on this planet. As the ignited soul seeks truth, you are acutely aware of the fact that you can no longer make choices from the intellect alone; rather your choices are a combination of intellect, intuition, heart, and communion.

So near you can feel it. Burning, as your flesh stings to stretch as birth happens. The woman reaches down and touches the head of her unborn. Suspended between worlds, there is a rush of ecstasy. It is during this moment that all the power of the universe flows through you.

This is Truth: **All the power of the Universe flows through you as you are about to be born (give birth)**. Staying present, conscious, awake, and in your power is imperative throughout this journey. For to come all this way, and in the end have it taken from you is like a butterfly beginning to emerge from her cocoon and someone coming along and helping her unravel her wings. We all know what happens to that butterfly.

This is no joke – you must find this power and claim your soul (or maybe you are claimed by your soul). Unfurl your wings and express your soul's calling. Choose consciously who is present during this critical period of birth. I do recommend only being witnessed by those who love you and can stand back, in awe, as you break through. You want no one meddling during this time, distracting you, taking your power away, and telling you what you should be doing. You only want a surrounding of love.

BIRTH

The moment of birth is a peak experience in life. Moments prior to birth, the mother and baby are flooded with the hormones called: Oxytocin and Catecholamine. Oxytocin is responsible for bonding, falling in love, and contracts soft tissues (such as the uterus). Catecholamine, from the adrenaline family, is responsible for awaking the mother so that she is hyper present, has the energy to push (and run and hide if needed) also, has eyes wide open to receive her baby. To receive the *light*.

We are deprived of these natural hormones when we are disturbed during this significant time of birth. Receiving this full hormonal cocktail at birth helps to facilitate healthy bonding and attachment. It has been suggested that oxytocin may be the necessary ingredient for supporting and encouraging a heart-based society; I concur.

Having said all of this, one might ask how this applies to their own Soul birth. If these hormones (Oxytocin, Endorphins, Catecholamine), when fully expressed during birth, increase the ability to love, bond and nurture, then it is probable that they are also present during the peak experience of an internal soul-transformation.

If this is truth (and I know I experienced a similar hormonal high during my soul labor) then I am proposing that it is strongly encouraged that we face our internal chaos with consciousness; from this undisturbed and quantum midwifery paradigm. This does not mean left alone without care or nurturing, but rather, that we are entrusted to find our inner power and give birth to our soul without someone else telling us *how* to do it.

After a deep grieving session, after totally letting go; I noticed that I would experience expansion, space and utter peace. The experience was so similar to that of labor – It actually blew my mind. I knew that Oxytocin was present and so were endorphins, which gave me that natural high, a feel-good sensation and the stamina to keep on going. My heart felt expanded and open; wide open.

What I am questioning is this: Is the hormone Oxytocin present and emitted during the experience of Grace?

There is a power in the room after one has given birth, a sacred presence, and reverence. This is a Divine experience, even if you do not believe in the Divinity. To witness this quality of birth you cannot help but silence yourself in awe and realize that you are walking on holy ground.

This new mother knows something, something that you can never know. Therefore, you are humbled in her presence.

The same holds true for your Soul Birth. When you are near someone who has walked through the tunnel of despair and has found their power, you sense that they carry a *knowing*. There is a calm presence about them, a solid Being and a grounded force within – you feel comfort being near them.

Birth is a pinnacle moment, the exhalation after all that work, the ultimate release. You have built up all this energy, worked harder than humanly possible, expanded and stretched in distorted ways, faced intensity and pain with unwavering presence and in the final push, you ecstatically let go and gave birth to that which was **dying to be born**.

You experience the flood of love and grace that *forever* changes you.

A cellular change has occurred, like that of a caterpillar to a butterfly. The old self has died along the way (and necessarily so) and a new sense of self has been born. This soul-self is larger than you are; it is motivated from an interior world that is alive and flourishing.

In this way everything changes, and life takes on a different meaning. You walk differently, all of you is with you. And you know what you have claimed: Your soul.

THE *Return*:
IMMEDIATE POSTPARTUM

A transformation has occurred. *Both mother and child experience a period of re-integration and re-organization. This stage may take about 5 to 10 minutes and is similar to the Quiescence in it's calmness and quietude. Mother and baby are stabilizing – reorganizing molecular structure – and neither may do anything that is visibly apparent for a few moments.- Whapio*

The Immediate Postpartum

The statement *"Do not disturb the immediate postpartum"* rings loud and true, as I sat and witnessed a soul birth the other night. I am reminded of Michel Odent again and the importance of the immediate postpartum. Accordingly, the first hour after birth, is considered to not only be the immediate postpartum, but the most sacred. During this time, a mother and baby have been exposed to the highest amounts of Oxytocin they will ever experience and deep bonding and attachment are taking place.

This is a *holy* time.

During this time, something is shifting on a cellular level. Information is being downloaded and the mother is still wide open, the 'veil is thin' between the tangible world and the unseen world. When met with a holy moment, what do you normally do? I hope that you silence yourself and open up to absorb the moment. I hope that you engage the meditative space with absolute presence and awe. This is not the time to take charge or interject your agenda. There is nothing rational about a holy moment.

When we disturb holy space, we are meddling with Life itself, so to speak. It makes me want to scream and swear profanity all over the place. I am speaking to those of us who are caregivers. You may be a caregiver of birth, or you may be an alternative healing practitioner, a counsellor, a minister, a shaman, a priestess, a midwife, I am speaking to anyone who stands witness to human transformation.

Remember, this is not your birth. This is not your journey. This is not the time for you to take charge of the 'scene'. **You are the witness**.

I have seen this repeatedly. The birth process has come to its peak and been fully expressed, and then there is this rush in the room, a need to take charge and disturb the completion of this process. This sacred window is the time of integration. It is a mistake to think that there is something that you need to be 'doing', aside from standing back to witness the process unfold, in honour.

It is a privilege to be present to this time of transformation. **Humility is of the essence**.

Rushing this highly sensitive time has been one of the causes of postpartum complications. When the immediate postpartum is disrupted with routine protocol, the flow of powerful helpful hormones are negatively affected. The room needs to be hot, dark, relaxing and calm, with a nurturing loving presence. If you stand back and witness this miracle, you can feel divine energy flowing through the mother and child - all the while still attached to the umbilicus.

There is no need to rush this process.

Your most important work at this time is to protect this sacred space, to allow a full integration to occur, to be meditative and listen deeply. Taking in the beauty and the awe of knowing that you have just touched *home*.

THE RETURN: THE ACQUISITION AND *Communion*

The period of Return and of Acquaintance are **times when distractions should be kept to a minimum** in order to respect the initial bonding between parents and baby. Stethoscopes, flashing cameras, suctioning devices, hands and voices other than the mother and father can be disruptive and inappropriate during these vital first few minutes, especially if the parents want the sanctity of the bonding process honored.- Whapio

Shortly after the immediate postpartum a new mother is eager to share this baby with her close community. It begins with her immediate family and/or those who were present at the birth.

The mother has a glow about her that is like no other, the birth glow I call it. This is a very contagious time and all who are near feed off this energy. Beaming in light, yet to fresh to venture out into the world.

It is critical that you choose wisely, whom you share your experience with. As excited as you are to share our new birth with your community and family, one might ask; "Who do I trust?" "Who do I love?" "Who loves me?" and "Who has believed in me?". Deeper yet, who has earned the honour to share in my new light.

Remember you have worked very hard, you have overcome obstacles beyond what your mind thought possible, you found your way through the desert terrain, you shed tears of pain, you faced your demon, you listened to your Soul's voice, you found new strength and purpose in your life – who do you want to share this with?

I encourage sharing with those who can experience your joy and not feed fear; or feed off your new *light*. Share with those who have loved you, those who have cared for you in ways you needed, those who listened without judgment and those who never abandoned you nor disturbed you. Nevertheless, share your story, your joy, your raw newness, your fragile new life wisely in the beginning.

During this time, you are still fragile. You are newly born and cells are reorganizing within your interior. This is a sacred postpartum time for healing and regaining of strength and health. You have exerted so much, endured so much, and lost an enormous amount of Chi, there is no rush to re-enter the exterior world. Often, new Mother's are encouraged to get back into the world immediately afterbirth.

I question this trend in our industrialized nations. It is detrimental to all to encourage a quick postpartum so one can 'get back to work'. Aside from the fact that the body is healing and becoming a new normal again, there is also a need to regain all the life force that was exerted. North America struggles with high rates of postpartum depression, and yet few are questioning the birthing practices and the postpartum rituals (or lack of rituals) women are experiencing.

Imagine for a moment having exerted so much energy, endured so much pain, and traversed so many terrains of hardship, to then immediately jump into the old world without any time for integration? You need and deserve to be nurtured, tended to in loving care, and encouraged to regain your health and strength so that you can bring your newfound Being into the world. It is a time of opening to receiving.

I encourage you to take a moment and consider how that would look for you.   .

Each day you find more strength and you know you are almost ready to bring this newborn Self into the extended community, eventually to the planet.

WEAVING THE STORY

The altered state is still apparent but beginning to close. How quickly it closes depends on how soon the mother returns to her ordinary reality. During this time, family and caregiver revisit the events of the birth. This is a crucial time of witnessing and articulating the journey to each other. Mother has an opportunity to review her altered state with her companions and formulate her wisdom. Partner is incorporated into the experiences and the parents share their insights. **The Weaving goes on forever**.-Whapio

There is power in telling our story and others take strength from those words. How you share, depends on what your soul's call is. However, it is always a craft of some sorts, a creative expression. For some, they may share their experience through the art of storytelling, others singing, poetry, writing, visual art, or dance. We all carry a story, sacred to our soul, and often we keep that story locked away. Whatever the belief is that silences our soul, it is time to disconnect from it and share with others.

Many women, after they have given birth in an empowering way, feel overwhelmed with joy and a desire to share with the world what they just experienced. The midwife who stood witness and guarded the birth space also carries a sacred piece of the birth. She, as the witness, knows the story from a different angle and therefore will always carry the story within her heart. These stories weave together a tapestry of life and birth and death. They are to be retold so that we can gain wisdom and courage from them.

As you share your story, notice how it is received. If it is coming from your soul, few will resist the power of it. Invisible teachings will be offered to those who are open to receiving guidance. We are always journeying and growing, it is through this kind of giving and receiving that we learn from one another. When times are hard, yet again, we reach into our satchels and remove a nugget of wisdom.

There is no beginning and end, life is a continuous circle and spiral, which is ever expanding. Along the way, you awaken, and gather experiences to place it in your life's sacred pouch. You keep these memories, stories, and experiences close to your heart. You remember that many have gone before and many will go after; we are all connected and your life's path is important.

Chisel away at all that you have experienced and eventually you will find your gold, and then share your gold essence with others. This gold is the wisdom within your wounds. In the sharing, you are removing unnecessary pebbles along the path, obstacles that stand in the way for others. This is a way to serve others and in return, you feel a sense of purpose greater than your ego could imagine.

Consider these questions: What story do you have to share? What story do you want to share? How do you tell your story? What is holding you back from sharing your story?

THE MOTHER

Gone.

      Underground.

            Forbidden.

                  Hidden.

Every day we give birth
We, women are giving
Birth to ourselves
As Mothers.

And the Mother is nowhere to be found.

We are lost.

      Without hope.

            Without Soul.

Where has *She* gone?

From Wounded to *Wise*

I fought and kicked and fasted and prayed and cursed and cried myself to the point of existing." ~ Alice Walker

FULL CIRCLE TO CLOSE THE GAP

The process of healing is one of reclaiming your internal power, stopping patterns that no longer serve, questioning your thoughts, asking for help when needed, learning humility and grace, learning how to grieve, and consciously choosing a different life course. It is a journey of deep interior investigation, peering into the soul and discovering parts of you that have been neglected, wounded, and silenced. It is a process of being undone and going from a place of giving a shit about all of the 'wrong' things, to giving a shit about all of the 'right' things.

Physiologically, healing occurs in the organs, bones, marrow, muscles and tissue of the body. Mentally and emotionally, healing occurs in the nervous system, which affects the entire function of the system. Soulfully, healing creates a union between the interior world and the exterior world. Spiritually, healing is about inspiration and devotion. Healing is regenerating health on all levels of being.

Healing is always happening and always available; we are graced with healing. It is all around; with each changing season you are shown this truth.

Each season, there is a death and a renewal, and you are gifted the wisdom to know that this too is true for humans.

Healing is hard fucking work, period. It invites you to visit the trenches of your soul, encounter your lost parts, experience the remorse over the choices you have made and the impact they have had, face the pain and shame that you have kept at bay and make new, often frightening choices that will shift your life as you know it. Is it any wonder that few of us have consciously chosen to heal at this deep level? So I ask, what is the internal driving force that encourages you to take on this journey with soul's a blazing?

As with labor, I believe we need a major catalyst to set this process in motion; for we would not intentionally *will* this quality of experience consciously. I believe strongly, that there is cellular knowledge that 'knows how' to heal thyself. The challenge we face is that the mind and ego, get in the way of the process of growth and transformation; these parts believe they can control this deeply programmed human nature.

Journal Entry

I thought I knew something about something. I thought that being 'educated and to be educated' meant you could say with conviction that you knew something about something. I thought I understood birth; that I could just teach what I had learned and experienced, that *this* was enough.

I was wrong.

Knowledge is ever expansive and expanding. Just when you think you have grasped a concept, another one comes along to be considered...and then another one, layer upon layer. We begin small and narrow minded, only considering that which is within the frame of your worldview. But like a concentric circle, you step outside of that worldview to include another one, and now you have expanded your consciousness.

This seems to be happening at such a rapid rate these days that I am losing grip on that which I thought I knew. I'm afraid to enter the land of no-mind. To let go of all that I have worked towards. Spent thousands to declare that I know something about something. Sure, biological sciences can tell us some facts about our body system. And yet, even within organic sciences we are still expanding on that which we declared as fact. Like the fact that Trees scream when they are murdered, and biology communicates with its community. Fact is fact until proven differently.

We are raised to know something about something, but maybe we are to practice not knowing when we declare we know we are close to the opportunity to expand our awareness even further. Yet, to not know leaves us in a state of profound insecurity. It is a paradox; to live in a state of open receptivity without the need to claim or declare anything as concrete knowledge. This is the feminine principle. Even the pursuit of knowledge as a commodity is a product of patriarchy. To remain open and receptive is viewed as disempowering and puts one at risk of being hurt; being lesser than.

To experience is to know only in the moment. Momentarily.

We can't celebrate another because we are perishing; we are void of our depth. We have lost our way. And we want what we can't have. We want what's in another. We want to fill the void, the soulless interior abyss. Striving. More striving. Do more. Be more. Get more. We hate it, yet we are consumed by it. It is the great addiction – The devastation of the soul.

When people are depressed, they suffer. And the word is dark, and everything is horrible, and some can't climb out and it is very scary. This is true. It is very scary to be living with the anguish of mental chaos – read: illness. But we want to use our sickness as a crutch. 'I'm this way because,' 'I'm sick because,' 'I did that because'... I needed the sickness to excuse my way of Being in the world.

Who do you want to be? What do you want to feel?

I am not sure we will win this battle. I am not sure we are supposed to – the human battle that is. The little girl in me is irritated. Patronized. And I'm supposed to rise above this oppression and not hold men (humans) accountable. Fuck that. What would holding them accountable look like? Our emotions are used as a weapon against us – the feminine.

You need to hand this over to the *Great Mother*.

It's okay. You can do it.

She's been with you always; she has been guiding you. Shining through you. Trust in her. Trust that your work is *Her* work. You've done good work. Truly. You can relax now; let go. You have worked so hard for a long, long time. You are allowed to receive now. The gifts of plenty. The fruits of your labour. This is *Her* work. She's working through you; She's *working* you. The Great Mother. *Her*. The

Cosmos; She's working through you. She's using you for good. To spread a message of love. To speak to the Mothers.

She doesn't give a fuck about the details. **The Great Mother *is* Life**. Alive. Angry. Love. The tides are turning, and She needs to come through. She will take care of you. Keep listening; stop trying. Keep acting on inspiration and keep loving. Be present. That *is* it.

Eventually, I saw that no one is actually drowning; it is all an illusion. We/they think they are drowning because we/they are believing the movie they are watching; the movie they are in. Awareness itself can see this. There is nothing awareness needs to do. It doesn't need to save anyone. This is one big virtual reality game we are in and we are all playing the players in the game. **When we die, we wake up to realize we never really died in the first place**. I suffer when I think that this reality is real, when I believe the stories I tell myself. Period. Trauma-land is too big. If we think we can fix it or prevent it, we will go mad. Triggers are inevitable.

Like labour we stay with the rise and fall of the sensations and ride it out.

There I am, in the belly of trauma-land. Like Jonah in the belly of the whale. And I've been given the torch of the skull. Baba Yaga's gift of initiation. The skull holds my power and lights my way; the way for others who are in the Belly. I've been asked to shed light on the Belly of trauma. Its an honour and a great task. Not for the faint of heart. And, not to be given away foolishly.

Rather, to be valued and honoured as a reminder, a badge of bravery and hardship. Triumph. As a reminder that the land of trauma incinerates you. As a reminder of the amount of sifting and sorting you've done.

As a knowing that I've earned my soul and my soul has earned its place.

I've been tested. And, I think I passed the test. My bright shining skull is a symbol of valour. Let us not sugar-coat trauma-land with heady science jargon. Trauma is the terrain of the soul. It is the soul's quest to journey through the muck. The Skull is the Holy Grail, and it's an extension of my Life Force. If I give it away, or hand it over with ease – all the secrets – I am doing others a disservice.

You must earn your Skull.

I am so bloody and clear that I've dropped into the terrain of the Soul now. **All there is, is Soul**. Never again will I foolishly devalue how hard I have worked to earn my place and my Skull. It's not ego – It's Soul. There is a difference.

Trauma-land is not pretty. It's a fucking mind-field. Full of traps and quicksand. If we are not careful, Trauma can swallow you up. That is it. Human existence as we have known it, has been trying to map out the territory of Trauma-land. Trauma is alive. A being in and of itself. She is the underworld, the pain of labour, the lava of the volcanos, the frozen lands, the fields of skulls, the valley of death.

Trauma traps our soul and robs it of life force.

Trauma is neither good nor bad.
She just *is* a part of the human story.
She is the initiator of the Soul's journey, home.

You do not heal from trauma by someone doing something for you. OMG, you only heal from trauma when you *claim* your lost Soul. *You* need to claim it! *No one can do this for you.* No teacher. No modality. No Healer.

You.

Need to call your spirit home and declare your soul. Your desire *to be alive* has to scream loud enough that you are willing to die for *Life Herself.*

SHE

She was banished a long time ago
Wild and reckless
Careless and free

She was.

Shunned and scolded
Taunted and tamed
Domesticated for safe keeping
Tucked away; far away.

Demanded to come out and play
The one who is the cast away
She is not welcome here
She is dangerous beyond keep
Tame her; claim her.

The voices of the over culture
Alive inside, she awaits
The calling
A longing to come home
She cannot; ought not
To be trusted.

Too *Red*

Hot

Holy

Holy is her name
See me, whole
Whore; holy.

Adorn me
Celebrate me
Honour me
I am
Life itself.

Call me home
Damn it
I want to be
Known.